D1038694

Wingtips for Women:
Success Without Compromise

Emma W. Morris

Emma Morris
I Cor 5:20

WINGTIPS FOR WOMEN: Success Without Compromise

Published by JEM Group, Inc.
Atlanta, GA
Copyright © 2010 by Emma W. Morris

International Standard Book Number: 978-0-9816582-0-9
Library of Congress Control Number: 2008935368
Printed in the United States of America

ALL RIGHTS RESERVED

Creative Direction by: Jeanette Bryce
Designed by: Diann Durham

No part of this publication may be reproduced, stored in a retrieval system, or transmitted, in any form or by any means—electronic, mechanical, photocopying, recording, or otherwise—without prior written permission.

For information:

JEM Group, Inc.
Atlanta, GA
www.morris-group.com

At last—a book for women who want to succeed without compromise. *Wingtips for Women* offers a candid conversation with women who have been in the trenches, succeeded personally and professionally and who are passionate about passing what they have learned to the next generation. Learn what Baby Boomers, Generation X and Millennials have to learn from each other about building great organizations. Gain practical tips for implementing successful mentoring and coaching programs to ensure the next generation of leaders.

About the Author

Emma W. Morris started her career as a math teacher to seventh-grade girls, an experience she believes inadvertently taught her much about sales. She went from teacher to IBM sales representative to her first entrepreneurial assignment. Emma has continued to alternate between large public companies and start-up ventures, always counting on her sales and sales leadership skills. Her early studies and work abroad gave her a love of other cultures, a gift that has stood her well in merger and integration work with large multi-nationals. She serves on numerous boards, both for-profit and not-for-profit, and is a sought-after mentor. When she is not traveling or cycling, she lives in Atlanta, Georgia with John, her husband of 30-plus years.

To John, my best friend and greatest fan.

TABLE OF CONTENTS

CHAPTER 1

Introduction

Are you among the 5 million female sales professionals in America today? [1] *Are you a woman on the top rung of the sales ladder? Do you aspire to the top job in sales? Do you sometimes dream of leading a sales organization, and then talk yourself out of pursuing that dream? Maybe you are the CEO who seeks to find a strong female sales executive to give your organization a competitive edge. If you are one of these fast-track professionals, this book is written for you.*

Between the covers of this book awaits the most cogent summary of collective tribal knowledge yet collected on the subject of female sales leadership. Through the lenses of 18 female chief sales executives of mid- to large-market public and private companies, representing a range of industries, the reader sees first-hand the harsh realities and

---

[1] "101 Facts on the Status of Workingwomen," Business and Professional Women's Foundation, October 2007, 2.

the simple joys that women experience on their way to the executive suite. Inside, you will find revealing, true stories from the front lines of business, related by women who cleared a path through the corporate minefield so that others can avoid the same obstacles and excel in the field of sales management.

Our purpose in searching out these personal accounts is two-fold: to inspire talented females who feel called to advance to the executive level of sales, as well as to educate hiring decision-makers, including CEOs, about the unique strengths that women bring to this level of leadership. It is not our intent to present a statistical report on the state of women in sales leadership. Such benchmarking studies are available elsewhere. What has not been broadly shared is the tribal knowledge heretofore only passed along to the next generation in one-on-one conversations and mentoring situations.

The oral sketches in the following chapters document the journeys of a rare group of amazing women who overcame numerous obstacles on the climb up the male-dominated sales ladders of large corporations. However, the principles for sales success they describe apply with equal impact to virtually all executive functions of any organization, large and small.

Moreover, from a big-picture view, these compelling recollections reveal an issue deeper even than widespread gender bias in the workplace. They document a disturbing aspect of how we fail to utilize and develop a significant segment of the available human potential in the United States. Given the fact that men and women possess equivalent levels of intelligence, the historical predisposition not to hire females in leadership roles vastly under-utilizes the potential contributions of millions of women—an astonishing oversight. Females represent more than one-half of the U.S. population and over 60 percent of the adult work force. A talent pool of literally over one-half of the U.S. population remains virtually untapped.[2]

Now, amid accelerating changes in demographics, global competition and the economy, leading-edge companies understand that they need all the brain power they can find. They also realize that women bring strengths to the sales force that many men lack to keep things in balance today and for the long haul. The battle survivors recounting their stories on the following pages, the author included, want to provide young women some of the tools they will need to take as full advantage as possible of this burgeoning change in traditional sales hiring.

The Final Frontier

In our tough economic times, pressure on CEOs to excel comes from all directions. Customers demand lower costs and higher value for products and services. Investors, shareholders, independent boards, business partners and employees all demand share price appreciation.

To build value and increase share price, CEOs turn to their chief sales executives to finesse two important levers—revenue and earnings growth. With such a pivotal role, the chief sales officer stands second only to the CEO as the most influential and highly compensated business leader.

However, the top sales level also carries a different kind of distinction which should serve as a warning sign to business leaders, and it is this: *as the last bastion of nearly total male dominance in business,*

---

[2] U.S. Department of Labor, Bureau of Labor Statistics, Employment and Earnings, *2006 Annual Averages and the Monthly Labor Review,* http://www.dol.gov/wb/stats/main.htm (accessed October 10, 2007); 2007 Center for Women's Business Research, http://cfwbr.org/facts/index.php (accessed October 10, 2007).

the chief sales executive position often lags far behind every other major corporate function in achieving gender diversity. This imbalance deprives sales teams of female leaders who can, and often do, revitalize the power of relationships to turn the business around.

Importantly, females who aspire to top sales jobs need to understand that the demands of executive positions are not gender-specific. Yet, questions remain: Why do corporations traditionally overlook the female one-half of the work force when selecting the best person to lead a function or drive an organization's revenue? Do male CEOs intentionally overlook great female candidates? Or, do talented women choose instead to take themselves out of the running long before the executive search begins?

Our study shows that both dynamics are in play.

Research Results Overview

Three sections comprise this book.

Tomorrow Is Here describes current realities of the business world, lifestyle choices that female workers face and imminent work force changes.

The Female Strengths presents the substance of our research: the all-too-often unsung yet crucial attributes that women bring to the table to help their organizations succeed. In their own words, extraordinary women leaders reveal details, rarely so candidly discussed, about challenges that women sales leaders face daily.

Making It Happen provides a guide for optimizing the strengths of female leaders at a time when companies need to utilize the total spectrum of human talent in order to prosper in coming years.

The Research Parti¬pants

The following pages draw their authority from many hours of conversation with women who overcame challenges on their way to the top. The reader will discover a treasure trove of trusted contemporary advice about hiring, promoting and becoming a female chief sales executive, embroidered by a rich collection of entertaining, and at times frightening, tales from the inner sanctum of sales leadership.

If those profiled in this work can do it, so can the reader. And if the reader is already on her way, we can help her accelerate the process. The modest price of this book should earn her a high return on investment toward her dream job.

The current scarcity of female chief sales executives made planning and executing our research a true challenge. Yet, once we identified women leaders to interview, rarely did they turn down the invitation to participate. Why? At first, we surmised it might be ego. But as the women themselves point out, "What better way to mentor the next generation in a highly leveraged manner?" They see this book as a platform to share what they have learned about success in sales leadership with the next generation—mentoring en masse.

The women leaders we interviewed were, without exception, knowledgeable about their roles, dedicated to their companies, professional in demeanor, strong in character, sensitive to global issues, confident in their abilities, inspiring in their achievements and gracious in spending time talking with us. Use their hard-won knowledge to your advantage as you aim for that top sales leadership spot and, as you ascend the ladder during your career, remember to pass along your own insights to other young women. That continuity and snowballing of knowledge is the legacy these leaders see as their purpose for bequeathing you, the reader, the benefit of their accrued wisdom.

For their insights, anecdotes and advice, we offer our sincere thanks to these remarkable women:

Research Participants

1. Rebecca Bernson – *Senior Vice President*, National Accounts Sales, Automatic Data Processing, Inc. (ADP)

2. Karen Bressner – *Senior Vice President*, Advertising Sales, TiVo Inc.

3. Lisa Cutts – *Vice President, Sales*, Misys Healthcare

4. Mary Delaney – *Chief Sales Officer*, CareerBuilder.com

5. Beth Doherty – *Vice President, Sales*, Emdigo, Inc. (formerly *Director, North American Sales*, Sony Computer Entertainment of America)

6. Dr. Judith (Judy) E. Fick – *Vice President & General Manager, Worldwide Sales*, Unisys

7. Deb Gallagher – *Managing Partner*, Pinnacle Selling, LLC (formerly *Senior Vice President, Global Sales*, Inovis, Inc.)

8. Heidi Gautier – *Vice President, U.S. Commercial Operations*, Endocrine Business Unit, Genzyme Corporation

9. Colleen Honan – *Senior Vice President, Global Sales, Services & Solutions*, OneSource Information Services, Inc.

10. Anne Kaiser – *Vice President Sales*, Georgia Power, a Southern Company

11. Corrine Perritano – *Executive Vice President, Direct to Consumer Business,* Jenny Craig, Inc.

12. Cathy Perry – *Professional Certified Coach and Founder,* InwardBound Coaching (formerly *Vice President, Marketing, Bell Sports, Inc.*)

13. Stacey Reid – *Vice President, Sales,* Chantal Corp.

14. Michele Sarkisian – *Group Vice President,* Maritz Inc.

15. Nancy Sells – *Senior Vice President Sales Strategy and Implementation,* PR Newswire Association, LLC

16. Jocelyn Talbot – *Vice President, Sales,* RetirementJobs.com (formerly *Senior Vice President, Sales,* Monster.com)

17. Dorane Wintermeyer – *Vice President, Sales,* Regence Blue Cross Blue Shield of Oregon

18. Senior Global Sales Executive, large public IT firm (anonymity requested)

CHAPTER 2

My Story

I remember the first time I realized that men and women were perceived differently in the corporate world.

At home on Thanksgiving break from my new job, I was in the kitchen helping my mother make a traditional Southern recipe called "beaten biscuits." Appropriate for their name, one takes a wooden mallet and strikes the dough over and over to achieve the right texture and to incorporate air into the mixture. When baked, the result of this process produces a cross between a soda cracker and a baking powder biscuit—a sort of puffy cracker. As I vented my anguish that men in my business unit treated me as less capable than they, my mother said, with a frustrated swing down onto the dough, "I thought that I and my generation had overcome these hurdles for you and your sister's generation, but it seems you are facing the exact same challenges." With that, she passed the mallet to me and suggested a few hearty blows to get my own frustration under control.

In that job, I learned the hard way that men and women were expected to act differently and, more devastating to my ideal picture of corporate America, to achieve differently.

Thirty-plus years later, the subject of gender discrimination remains controversial. While there is non-stop research and dialogue about inequities between men and women in hiring, promotion and compensation, especially for leadership positions such as the chief sales executive, both men and women seem to remain stuck in somewhat intractable and opposing views.

Now, after years of being up to my earrings discussing women in leadership roles, I conclude that both sexes, as if by reflex, dig in their heels to defend their position instead of learning more about the topic—and possibly developing new insights and implementing positive changes. For many, accepting such a novel mindset would mean moving out of a comfort zone created by tradition, necessity and opportunity. Yet, by learning about and embracing the still unfolding notion of women in leadership roles, both men and women can sow the seeds of progress for themselves and their organizations.

Within that context, our research team began seeking facts and insights to fill the information void about how women overcome obstacles to achieve and succeed as business leaders, a triumph that continually mystifies men and women alike. This book documents that quest using the sales function as our learning laboratory.

My own story of growing up is one that still causes me to chuckle. It served to protect me from narrowing my horizons too early in my career, yet it also gave me a less than realistic expectation of how the world would see me as a woman on a fast-track career.

You see, my parents had the same educational background, Ph.D.s in physical chemistry, and taught in the same university at the same level. I did not know that most people's parents had separate and unique roles. At home, both my parents cooked, cleaned, helped with homework and packed lunches for four school-aged children. I was the eldest of the four—two girls, then two boys. I acquired the role of trendsetter for my siblings of both genders. My younger brothers came to me to learn to tie knots or build a fort, as well as to learn the finer arts of cooking an angel food cake as a surprise on Mother's birthday. No one had ever pointed out to me that boys could do things that girls could not.

Later, it was my seventh grade math teacher, Mrs. Haggard, who as a role model further solidified the concept in my young mind that girls can do anything that boys can do—period. A large and formidable woman whom you did not want to disappoint, she "cut no one any slack," boys or girls. She was also the most demanding teacher I ever had, but as is often the case, the one for whom I worked the hardest and whose good marks made me extraordinarily proud.

Much later in graduate school, with an average of 100 going into the statistics final exam, my professor recognized my ability with numbers and logic and steered me toward a career I had never even considered. A retired IBM executive, he exempted me from the rest of the semester and suggested I apply to IBM in sales.

With this new-found realm of career options laid before me, I was eager to demonstrate that I could be successful in the male-dominated world of computers. I appeared at my IBM interview prepared to talk numbers and dazzle the hiring manager with my mathematical acumen. However, to my surprise, we spent the entire time discussing the junior year of college I spent in France. He was more intrigued by my poise, flexibility and comfort level when faced with new and unique situations than in exploring my technical background. He offered me a sales job on the spot. A year later, during my performance review, he revealed his real reason for hiring me without any dialog surrounding my technical expertise. He heard, in my recounting of my year abroad, the ability to assimilate diverse bits of data, analyze them, eliminate irrelevant facts, and construct a viable solution.

Thus began my IBM experience, with its world-class training that served as a solid foundation for the rest of my business career. I continue to be indebted to that professor for pointing me in a new direction, and to that original hiring manager for seeing in me qualities that I did not even realize were valuable to success in the business world.

As a young IBM sales rep, I became the sole female survivor of my initial sales training class. It was lonely. One day an outside speaker came in to tell us how to dress to impress clients. I was excused from the rest of the session after he could not answer my question as to where to find five-pound wingtip shoes in ladies' sizes!

On the other hand, as a "cute young thing," I often gained entrance into industrial, testosterone-filled manufacturing plants where my male colleagues had failed to be admitted. But once inside, I still had to prove myself and sell my company's wares. The most effective method was to relate stories of how other IBM clients had used that hardware to increase sales, reduce waste, increase production or whatever was important to that prospect.

Sure, the company provided copious pages of statistics that I could leave behind for later reading, but it was the stories that had staying power. They were about real people and real successes, not lab results and promises that my male sales counterparts typically reverted to in their quest for a sale. Anecdotes resonated with my male audiences because they knew the numbers stood behind them. Using stories, I turned a fact-ridden product into an emotional, feeling experience. That was my natural style.

Ultimately, I came face-to-face with raw gender bias in the

workplace, and it was a rude awakening. Yet, I am grateful that I did not know about limitations set by society until I had already launched myself into the business arena. If I had been convinced as a young girl to lower my expectations, would I have chosen a less challenging occupation? Would I have settled for less and assumed it was my due? Perhaps.

Clearly, other female IBM sales reps have been successful. Today, IBM's sales force touts 40 percent women, well ahead of the industry standard of 25 percent for other high-tech employers.[3]

In a real sense, the concept of a successful female business leader stood as a contradiction to mainstream culture as played out in 1950s' television programs such as *Leave it to Beaver* and *Father Knows Best.* The prevailing cultural premise: the woman is first at home, the man is first at work; the woman is sweet, the man is wise.

Reflecting those ideals, many of my generation carry an indelibly etched picture of the successful "career woman." A female in the top sales leadership position must surely be a forceful, controlling, "b-word" sort of a woman, right? She takes and commands control over all facets of her life—she is in control at home and at work. To be a take-charge woman at work must surely mean her home life is a wreck. What self-respecting man would be married, long term, to such a strong woman? Obviously, her husband must be some oddity or weakling. Promote that successful career woman to the top sales executive in the organization, and all sorts of embellishments are added to that original image, none of them very flattering to womankind.

The reality is quite different from the image. Our research shows strong women leaders take time to have successful marriages, play with

[3] Bulkeley, William M. "Tech and Testosterone: A Data-Storage Titan Confronts Bias Claims," *Wall Street Journal,* September 12, 2007, A1.

their children, raise families and serve in the community. Meanwhile, many also take the time to share their tribal knowledge with the next generation of women leaders.

At the same time, we, both men and women, unwittingly seem to hold onto that 1950s' view of women as primarily homemakers and care givers. About 71 percent of American women who are also mothers do work in some professional capacity, whether inside or outside the home.[4] These women earn a "second," but not primary, income. When family commitments grow too heavy, the woman is usually the parent expected to drop or decrease her career obligations for the sake of the family. Today, when daycare centers and nannies beckon on every corner, rarely does childcare interfere with the mother's work life. The obstacles more likely come from other family situations, i.e., establishing a household, putting a spouse through professional school or caring for aging parents or in-laws.

Even today, that 1950s' perspective simmers in the background of our culture and seeps into hiring and developmental decision-making in the business world. Somehow, we have forgotten the strong women who quite effectively ran the country during World War II.

Yet, the traditional view obstructs the path of younger workers. If the hiring executive is evaluating these workers in light of his or her expectations of proper roles for men and women, there may be a disconnect for both parties. It may be difficult for an older business-person with more traditional views of men's and women's home and hearth roles to understand that younger workers may not be thinking about marrying and having the traditional 2.3 children. They may

---

[4] Economic Policy Institute, "Mothers at Work," *Facts and Figures*, http://www.epi.org/newsroom/releases/2005/05/05050_Mothers_Day_Facts.pdf.

not even be thinking about building a career, but rather, the next adventure. Jobs, to this new breed of employee, are often stepping stones to the next life experience, but not a rung on a career ladder.

A recent study found that when it comes to marriage, women of Generation Y (generally those individuals born after 1982 and commonly referred to as Millennials) are less conventional and more cynical than the men. In fact, it is the Millennial women who lead the generation's redefinition of marriage. Although these young women are eager to get married themselves, they are less likely to believe parents must be married, much more likely to question marriage as a way of life and more discouraged about prospects in their peer group—49 percent believing most of the men they know are not responsible enough to get married.[5] These attitudes will turn upside down the expectations of a hiring executive if he or she is not ready to think outside traditional roles for both men and women in this age range.

But there are other surprises for the older hiring executive. It is my privilege today to teach business courses to Millennial young people at a local college. My observation is that this generation does not have some of the basic business skills I expected to be well developed by this point in their education.

As the professor to business majors nearing graduation, I occasionally pose a deep question or make a profound statement about the topic at hand. When I do this, invariably a loud silence fills the room, punctuated by the quiet clicking of fingers over keyboards as students "Google" to find the answer or validate my statement. They do not even pause to contemplate an appropriate response before using

---

[5] Greenberg, Quinlan, Rosner and Polimetrix, *Coming of Age in America, Part II*, Washington, DC, 2005.

Google as a crutch. Instead, they instantly access their group-oriented technology to "percolate" an answer. If not accessing Google, they just as easily put a question out to their Facebook, MySpace or Twitter community to collaboratively arrive at a response. These are Millennials in action. They have no fear of contradicting me or embellishing my statement, based on what their Internet responses reveal.

Another disconnect between the mentality of my generation and the Millennial mindset recently struck me in full force. I met with a graduating business senior who planned a career in sports and entertainment sales and marketing. He had dressed for a meeting with me, one of his major professors, in his "best" tee shirt, shorts and flip-flops. He twiddled a toothpick in his mouth during our conversation. About halfway through the dialogue, I asked him, "If I were actually the person who could offer you a job, would you change anything about this interview?"

Astounded, he paused and considered the question, thoughtfully twisting the toothpick between his teeth. Eager to keep this conversation thread moving, I asked if he thought the toothpick might be something he could give up for a job interview. Yes, he finally agreed, he supposed the toothpick could go. We never got to the question of attire. It was my turn to be astounded.

I realized the basics of interview dressing had evaded this young man's realm of knowledge. His lack of perception was less about how to dress and act in an interview, and more about how to present oneself as an adult businessperson. He just did not get it! In subsequent classroom exchanges, I have come to realize that the female students are just as clueless as the males about what hiring managers deem to be a professional image.

Clearly, learning the basics will be essential for building a solid foundation for a successful career. The Millennials must realize that although their mode of attack on the business world is different from that of their predecessors, and may ultimately prove to be equally productive, getting the first "foot in the door" to wage that war involves interaction with already established professionals. It is not their peers who will be hiring these new graduates. Management will have a difficult time seeing past the seemingly lackadaisical, apathetic and disrespectful attitude evidenced by an unprofessional image, despite the individual's actual potential.

Although male and female Millennial workers *can* learn the basics of business and much more, with appropriate guidance, society continues to create environments outside the office that make it more difficult for female sales leaders to be effective, compared to the relative ease experienced by males.

Societal factors, along with an ingrained, historical preference for men in the workplace, stand as fundamental reasons why more women do not occupy top leadership positions, especially in sales. Societal norms reinforce a woman's natural affinity to nurture a family and keep the home fires burning. However, when those societal standards spill over into the work world, they present new challenges for aspiring female leaders. Top revenue-producing females are reluctant to pursue promotions due to the steeper, rockier grade they need to climb, often involving lower pay and sacrifices they will have to make at home. Globalization, 24/7 obligations and travel add to this challenge, and lines between professional and personal lives become blurred.

If you are among the approximately 5 million saleswomen in this country, hopefully this book will inspire you to set your course, put action to desire and position yourself for continued growth, advancement and success. If you are in a position to recruit or hire sales executives, our desire is that these stories will prompt you to gain new insights and seek out qualified females to revitalize your organization.

And, if you need the recipe for my mother's beaten biscuits, feel free to email me at *emorris@morris-group.com*!

Emma

Section One

TOMORROW IS HERE

CHAPTER 3

Welcome To The Real World

A key statistic noted in our Introduction is worth reiterating—
females represent more than one-half of the U.S. population and over 60
percent of the adult work force.[6] Equality of the sexes in the workplace
has been steadily gaining greater balance since the national battle cry
first reverberated in the 1960s. Why, then, do so few women hold senior
sales positions in private and public companies, a distressing truth that
exists in nearly all senior functions and across all industries?

Ask that question aloud in a crowded room, and one of two
reactions generally occurs—the buzzing conversation drops to a dead
silence, or the crowd comes to life with a cacophony of opinions.
Either way, the query evokes salient realities about the business world,
our American culture and, importantly, our innate strengths and
limitations as men and women.

Is it surprising that men view the concept of women in leadership
roles differently than do women? No. The surprise comes with the

---

[6] U.S. Department of Labor, *2006 Annual Averages*, 2007 Center for Women's Business Research,
(accessed October 10, 2007).

realization that both men and women often hold strongly divergent assumptions about the business acumen of women which have no basis in reality. This position inhibits both genders from learning more about each other and possibly developing new attitudes and behaviors.

The Way Things Are

Rare is the woman who weathers the arduous journey from the rank and file to the executive suite. As noted above, women account for over 60 percent of the U.S. work force, yet only about 16 percent of Fortune 500 senior leaders are female, according to a study by the Business and Professional Women's Foundation.[7] Therefore, men occupy more than five times the number of leadership positions than do women among the top 500 corporations in the country. Despite the advances women have made into the boardroom over the past several years, a distressing imbalance remains at the top of most organizations.

Use Your Brains!

BETH DOHERTY
Vice President, Sales
Emdigo, Inc.
(formerly Director, North American Sales, Sony Computer Entertainment of America)

Doherty grew up with two sisters and one brother, and her father worked as a union longshoreman. "My father challenged each of his girls to realize we might be girls, but that we had brains just like the guys," she recounts. "'You are all the same,' he would say, 'so use your brains!'"

Taking that advice to heart, Doherty went on to succeed in three careers. At Gap Inc., she improved productivity and helped to introduce the Gap Kids concept. She moved to a sales role at Sony, just in time for the launch of the hugely successful PlayStation. Next, she joined a company that became SoundBlast, helping to develop and market video games.

Putting her mind to work from a consumer perspective, Doherty has consistently been able to understand what consumers will want next.

---

[7] "101 Facts on the Status of Workingwomen," 2.

More specifically, according to the report, only 60 companies out of those top 500 had females filling more than a quarter of all senior management positions. Peel back these statistics, however, and a pattern emerges—a lack of women in leadership positions as a result of numerous social, economic and systemic pressures.

"Despite the Civil Rights movement and the women's movement, changes in every system level are needed, as equal access to opportunities in the workplace continues to elude women and minorities," writes Dr. Ellen Cook, professor of international business and accountancy at the University of San Diego. "The glass ceiling remains omnipresent, and many talented employees never reach their vocational goals because of their race or gender. Women struggling to take care of their families while earning a living must do so with little assistance from a system that regards family work as invisible, of secondary value and incompatible with paid labor practices. Many women continue to earn less than men do, and they are less likely than men are to get assistance from their partners with the work that still must be done after the paid work is completed."[8]

Women, much more so than men, embrace their multiple roles as spouse, parent, executive, mentor and more, and make calculated choices in favor of one role over another during the life of a sales career. In some cases, women choose to stay with a good employer who knows their skills and successes, and is willing to invest in them for the future. These women may suffer in the long term income-wise for the pay disparity between sales manager and chief sales executive (as much as

---

[8] Ellen P. Cook, Mary J. Heppner and Karen M. O'Brien, "Career development of women of color and White women: assumptions, conceptualization, and interventions from an ecological perspective - Special Section," *Career Development Quarterly*, June 2002.

100 percent in some cases).[9] The positive trade-off is that both parties are working with a known entity, thus avoiding the risk of losing a proven and profitable synergy within the company. Typically, these women stay in this role longer than the men at the same level, which is good news for the executive, the company and its shareholders.[10]

Regardless of the so-called liberation of women, there remain a number of household chores relegated to the woman of the home seemingly by some unspoken agreement on the part of the women themselves, as well as the men in their lives—whether at home or at the office, and regardless of the rank or position of the woman at the office. Does that mean we are to believe that women are not at the top rung of the career ladder because they are still juggling multiple roles on every rung of that ladder? Is the juggling act made more challenging by their belief that each role deserves their best and total effort? Is it possible to simultaneously be the best mom, the best wife and the best executive? Our study indicates an emphatic yes to each of these questions. Most of the women in our study are in long-term marriages, have one or more children, and many of those children are still at home and as active in sports, church and hobbies as any other normal "kid next door." These women have learned to juggle their roles at every rung along the way to the executive suite. We will examine in a later chapter the specifics of how they perform their juggling act.

The Sales/Marketing Conundrum

Focus in all facets of home and work, however, is a key to the success of these women. On the career front, our study seems to

---

[9] *Sales Benchmark Index*, "World Class 100 Report," survey of 3,700 U.S. publicly traded companies across 19 industries from 1996-2006.

[10] *Sales Benchmark Index*, survey.

demonstrate that "married moms" who focus their careers solely on sales and not even the commonly lumped together "sales and marketing" role can be even more successful sales executives.

Like a pair of twins, the disciplines of Sales and Marketing brazenly skip hand-in-hand through the rugged terrain of Customer Land, confident that if one should fall the other will be there to help, and no one can tell them apart, anyway. Unlike human twins however, Sales and Marketing do not always know what the other is thinking. The differences become real when a sales professional takes on the role of marketing and the execution of the company's marketing strategies is derailed by a lack of relevant knowledge.

For the woman striving to get ahead, this sales-or-marketing divergence on the path to success can cause confusion and doubt to replace buoyant self-confidence. But she must make a choice and move on. At least, that is what Deb Gallagher did.

Now managing partner of Pinnacle Selling, LLC, Gallagher learned the ropes of both sales and marketing during her 22-year career at Management Science America (MSA), 10 of which involved executive sales management. That dual experience resulted in more than a sound bite on her résumé; it helped her identify her true calling.

"I feel I've not been truly effective in marketing roles," Gallagher confides. "I am intelligent and strategic enough to have executed some marketing activities and deliverables, but I am a saleswoman. My DNA is sales. I have resisted taking on marketing responsibilities as I have become a more proficient sales executive.

"I have been promoted because, number one, I love sales and, number two, the performance comes specifically from who you are. I'm fortunate to have been able to demonstrate influence in both sales and management leadership."

In Search of Chief Sales Executives

One surprising data point grabbed our attention. While female corporate executives are represented more or less evenly among functions such as finance, operations, information technology and human resources, only a microscopic 1 percent of those women hold the critical post of chief sales executive.[11]

This finding carries weight, because after the chief executive officer, the chief sales executive often has the greatest impact on the company's bottom line. While the CEO owns the strategy and vision for the organization, there is little bottom-line value without a chief sales executive driving revenue. If that sales executive delivers, the rest of the company has a job to do. Without customers and the constant stream of revenue-producing sales they generate, there is no company. As an incentive for assuming this critical role, the chief sales executive frequently enjoys the second highest compensation in the company.

Historically, females gain promotions and perform well in numerous types of corporate leadership roles. However, this success is not the case in the critical and lucrative function of sales. Our research reveals that it takes much longer for women to reach the top spot in sales, and that females fail or leave the job much more frequently than males. There are many causes for this imbalance. One reason may be men's willingness to "job-hop" more frequently than women.

Male chief sales executives change jobs on average every 19 months to advance their career and compensation. With every move, their income typically increases upward of 20 percent, plus stock options when available. Males tend to reach the top sales management

---

[11] "101 Facts on the Status of Workingwomen," 2.

role between the ages of 38 and 42 years.[12] Based on this data, and assuming men begin their careers upon graduating from college at 22 years old, they take an average of 16 to 20 years to reach the top. Women, on the other hand, change jobs much less frequently. They tend to stay in a single organization and grow their way to the chief sales executive position. For the few women who eventually make it, our field interviews show the average age of these female chief sales executives to be 48 to 52 years.

Deb Gallagher believes that female sales executives have more than longevity in the job going for them and their employers. She postulates that women sales leaders actually have the upper hand over their male counterparts in terms of characteristics and traits more innate to women. "We are empathetic; we are good listeners," Gallagher says. "I think we are better collaborators, and we have stronger communication skills. Customers are willing to see us because we are women, and it's easy to impress them if we show we are competent and prepared."

However, it is not all roses. She adds, "Women have disadvantages. We often do not have the business acumen that men generally acquire sooner and more often than women. The same holds true with sports knowledge [which is a time-tested common discussion topic during sales encounters with clients or prospects]. Finally, don't forget the overall comfort factor of men gathering with their own gender."

Smart Moves

Those who inhale the rarified atmosphere of executive office do not magically receive the insights of wisdom, integrity or power.

---

[12] *Sales Benchmark Index,* survey.

Along with the glitz of status, higher pay and executive perks, senior executives, whether in the private or the public realm, must actually work long and hard—perhaps even longer and harder than their male counterparts—to achieve difficult goals in order to remain on top.

To fulfill their roles successfully, both men and women executives can be expected to sacrifice personal obligations from time to time. Chief financial officers regularly burn the midnight oil preparing quarterly earnings reports or crunching numbers during a merger or acquisition transaction. Chief information officers agree to service levels with 99.999 percent uptime commitments that place them perpetually on call. Directors of manufacturing, benchmarked against their peers, land on the front page of the *Wall Street Journal* for a product recall, further ramping up the job's intensity and level of stress.

The need clearly has never been greater for leaders who can simultaneously strategize, visualize, execute the vision and inspire employees. Indeed, finding the right people to join and lead a company now outranks all other concerns of business leaders, according to results of the "2008 Top Five Total Rewards Priorities Survey," sponsored by Deloitte Consulting and the International Society of Certified Employee Benefit Specialists. Survey participants identified "talent management" as their single most critical organizational challenge. The urgency surrounding talent issues bumped "cost of rewards programs" out of the top priority spot in the survey it had held for the past nine years.

Popular wisdom holds that only a courageous CEO will take the risk of naming a female as chief sales leader. But, more than simply a courageous act, bringing a woman to that pivotal role can be a very smart business move. A female as head of sales can provide unique and sorely needed strengths to the job in terms of people skills and long-view perspectives. She also serves as a compelling point of differentiation for the company, which can lead to unanticipated windfalls such as attracting a wider pool of diversity in the applicants to other senior positions, increased attention to the company by the media as a forward-thinking innovator, and inroads into previously untapped client opportunities. There may also be a new and expanded network of local and national professional, civic and charitable organizations interested in wooing the attention of the new "horse of a different color."

If a CEO is willing to take the risk, what are the advantages of naming a female chief sales executive? What value does she add? Is the controversial decision worth it? What are the costs of such a move? Are there any disadvantages, and if so, are these real or only perceived?

Until now, an objective, independent investigation did not exist to answer those questions, and CEOs had virtually no examples to follow. The histories revealed by the pioneering women in the following chapters are intended to fill that void.

CHAPTER 4

Lifestyles

As part of living, everyone makes lifestyle choices. Some choices are deliberate and planned, while others occur as a result of circumstances. People make decisions to obtain or change a job, to stoke the home fires, to go to school or to follow a passion. Lifestyle choices may be influenced by external pressures—societal norms, family obligations, finances, traditions, circumstances and abilities—but at the end of the day, every person stands responsible for selecting his or her own course.

The work world magnifies the significance of lifestyle choices, and these choices quite often differ for men and women. While employment provides the means to enjoy a certain quality of life and to achieve personal fulfillment, one's occupation also consumes most of the available daily hours, often usurping time for family interaction or other life-enriching endeavors. Influences outside of the office can make it more difficult for women sales leaders to be effective at work as they strive to "do it all." Because senior level sales positions often require extensive travel and meetings outside the regular workday, the constant juggling of time can become overwhelming. Unless the woman feels comfortable with balancing all of the various aspects of daily living, each one vying for equal attention, guilt can creep in and influence good judgment. This fundamental issue of how to balance it all without living in a constant state of guilt and frustration seems to be one of the principal reasons more women do not pursue or occupy an executive position. Sometimes it is easier to opt out all together or to lower one's expectations and career aspirations. Clearly, the women in our study did neither. Instead, each has made a set of complex work and lifestyle choices over the lifetime of a very successful career.

According to Sylvia Hewlett, author of *Off-Ramps and On-Ramps*, more and more women are struggling with increasing demands at home and at work and are taking time off from work to be at home. More than 60 percent of career women are choosing this path, according to Hewlett. "But while they're doing so for 'pull factors' like time for children (45%) or for eldercare (24%), they're also motivated by 'push factors' such as unsatisfying work (29%) or feeling stalled in their careers (23%). Women are much more likely to respond to the pull of family," Hewlett concludes, "when they feel hemmed in by a glass ceiling."[13]

CEOs, recruiters, hiring managers and job candidates must candidly consider lifestyle preferences in order to make the best choices for their organizations. Otherwise, the powerful forces of work life and home life will continue to grind against each other like Earth's tectonic plates, creating tremors in the very quality of life these women aspire to achieve.

---

[13] Sylvia Ann Hewlett, "Off-Ramps and On-Ramps," interview by Melinda Morino during *Harvard Business Review* podcast on May 24, 2007; also in "Sylvia Hewlett on Helping Women Succeed," *WFC Resources*, June 2007.

More Choices

Changes in business, culture and technology continue to create new lifestyle options for men and women at all levels. Thanks to the global reach of the Internet, managers and employees alike can be "at work" anywhere, anytime. The virtual office continues to grow in popularity. Many companies encourage employees to telecommute by working at home all or a portion of their work week. More positions list part-time, short-term or flex-time options to give employers and workers more flexibility in organizing their daily schedules.

A growing number of men and women are working from home according to The Dieringer Research Group report, "WorldatWork 2006 Telework Trendlines." Significantly, more people who are married or living together tend to telework, thus giving more women at least the choice to pursue careers outside the home.[14] While this practice has been a growing trend over the last three decades, recent rapid advances in technology over the last ten years have enabled the rising tide of young and more technology-savvy workers to seamlessly incorporate teleworking into their lives. In the midst of these shifts, men and women business leaders slowly but surely accommodate more blended lifestyles, mingling traditional male-breadwinner and female-homemaker roles.

Nancy Sells, senior vice president of sales strategy and implementation and 19-year veteran of PR Newswire Association, LLC, tells her story: "My company is a terrific employer. We have great benefits and lower than industry average turnover across the board.

---

[14] The Dieringer Research Group, "WorldatWork 2006 Telework Trendlines™ Survey," summarized and edited online by Katie Hoynski, The Telework Advisory Group of WorldatWork, Fall 2006, University of Wisconsin-Eau Claire *Working*, http://www.workingfromanywhere.org.

We are known as a safe place for women who are trying to manage a career and a family. Yes, there were times when I had to pass even putting my hat into the ring because I knew my two girls had to come first. It was hard to see men who were not as well qualified get the job I knew I could have had. It was even more painful when those same men failed in the job I knew I could have excelled in. Fortunately, when I was ready to refocus on my career, the company supported me in the choices I made. The company knew me, and I didn't have to reprove myself to get a shot at the next rung on the ladder."

According to a 2004 report by the Hidden Brain Drain Task Force, a coalition of Fortune 500 companies concerned about the loss of women workers, at some point 37 percent of high-powered women (defined as women with graduate, professional or high-honors undergraduate degrees) choose to take time out of career pursuits to focus on family, whether for children or elderly parents. By comparison, the same report found that 24 percent of men voluntarily leave their careers at some point, but their reasons are typically in order to return to school or to switch to another job. The percentage of the women voluntarily taking time out who want to reenter the work force after a short break for family situations is a high 93 percent. Some 25 to 30 percent of this latter group will choose a longer break out of family necessity, but for women in senior roles today, career has become such a part of their identity that they feel compelled to return to work. When they do, it is not a return just to a job, but to a high-powered career.[15]

By choosing to leave work for family reasons and then return, nearly two-thirds of today's women leaders will have non-linear careers.[16] In contrast, men of the same age are able to proceed with

---

[15] Hewlett.
[16] Hewlett.

their careers as priority without interruption, only because women tend to be more willing to step out of work temporarily to address family obligations. Or, the female one-half of the couple may not necessarily be more willing, but the pair holds the traditional viewpoint that it is "more fitting" for the female part of the equation to take on the lion's share of family responsibilities. Even as women have commanded higher wages and have moved into more senior roles, studies show that the number of hours worked on the job by husbands has stayed about the same. However, the number of hours these men spend doing household chores has gone up 50 percent for married men (from 13 hours to 19 hours over the last 40 years).[17] Even with the support of a helpful mate, it seems that the adage "a woman's work is never done" may still be true!

The good news for women is that despite traditional ideology, they have more lifestyle choices than ever. The bad news is that the choices are not always easy or devoid of sacrifice.

Family Matters

The most frequent lifestyle choice for female workers is whether, when, or even if to begin a family. Ingrained Judeo-Christian views of family and marriage still include both a mother and father on the scene, living in harmony together. A recent Pew Research Center study on marriage and children found that 69 percent of Americans agree that children need both a mother and a father. However, more than one-third of all births in the U.S. are to unwed mothers, up from past

---

[17] John Knowles, "Why Are Married Men Working So Much? The Macroeconomics of Bargaining Between Spouses," *IZA Discussion Papers,* University of Pennsylvania and Institute for the Study of Labor (IZA), no. 2909, revised February 2008.

studies, and 71 percent of Americans view the increase in births to unwed mothers as a "big problem."[18]

Mother Nature entrusts the child-bearing responsibility exclusively to women. Although possibly involved in the initial decision regarding if and when to conceive, at least for the foreseeable future males cannot carry a child for nine months or deliver the child into this world. If a woman, or a couple, wants to have a baby, the woman usually must take at least some time away from work to do so. Inevitably, this results in some interruption in her career.

Following birth, children require on-going care and attention for everything from illness to daycare to extracurricular activities and, at times, educational or developmental issues. In short, at least one parent must be able to respond in person when their child gets sick or sent to the principal's office.

Complicating matters for female sales leaders age 40 or older, another factor looms: which partner in a marriage will take care of aging moms or dads? As parents live longer due to advances in geriatric healthcare, they often remain in their own home but still need periodic or even around-the-clock care. Sandwiched in between the needs of aging parents and growing children, women executives face new dilemmas and difficult choices as they try to be both breadwinner and caregiver. Nearly 60 percent of individuals caring for an adult over the age of 50 are simultaneously working, and the majority of those are employed full-time.[19]

---

[18] "The Fatherless Child," *Christianity Today*, October 2007, page 25, citing Pew Study, www.pewresearch.org/assets/social/pdf/marriage.pdf.

[19] "The MetLife caregiving cost study: productivity losses to U.S. business," MetLife Mature Market Institute & National Alliance for Caregiving, Westport, CT, 2006, http://www.pascenter.org/frames/pas_frame.php?site=http%3A%2F%2Fwww.caregiving.org%2Fpubs%2Fdata.htm (accessed April 25, 2007).

While these factors discourage many women leaders from having children or devoting time to family—children and/or parents, others manage to make both family and career commitments mesh harmoniously. Over 67 percent of highly-educated women in their 30s with a young child at home are in the labor force, as are 75 percent of women with a graduate degree and a child under age 18.[20] Despite the burdens of extensive travel and time spent on work-related matters outside regular business hours, almost all the top women sales executives we spoke with had successful, long-term marriages and children. Obviously, these couples have found working solutions that benefit everyone, children included.

For women especially, the issue centers more on life *choices* than on work/life *balance*, contends Mary Delaney, chief sales officer at CareerBuilder.com. Just as men do, women make choices about their careers, lifestyle and families. Tradition may lag behind some of the choices, but they are the women's decisions to make, she emphasizes.

Ideally, lifestyle decisions involving spouses or life partners should be made together, since the lifestyle

Make Lifestyle Choices

MARY DELANEY
Chief Sales Officer
CareerBuilder.com

Delaney brought to her job some career insights from Jack Welch, former chairman of General Electric Corp. Welch was never her direct boss, but early in her career he was the keynote speaker at Delaney's company's sales kickoff event. Welch advised the aspiring sales leaders that the life of a chief sales executive, male or female, is not about balancing work and life, but making choices about lifestyles.

---

[20] H. Boushey, "Are women opting out? Debunking the myth," Washington, DC Center for Economic and Policy Research, 2005, 11, http://www.cepr.net/publications/opt_out_2005_11.pdf (accessed January 28, 2006).

choice of one can limit or expand the choices available to the other. Unfortunately, among married couples with children, as of 2004, mothers are spending the same amount of time taking care of their children on days when they are working as they did 25 years ago.[21] However, many women we interviewed were married to husbands who chose the role of stay-at-home dad, or at least agreed to that arrangement for a certain time frame.

"My husband had to learn to throw birthday parties for first graders and braid little girls' hair, but he's great at it now," Delaney says. "We made the decision together, knowing we can switch roles again from time to time."

Along with the choice of *if* to have children, women often have the option of *when*. The timing of childbearing in her life cycle can have a direct impact on the progress of a woman's career. Indeed, women may be in a better position than ever to make timing decisions that can minimize career slowdowns. A woman having a child will need to step away from work temporarily, but she can control the timing—at least somewhat. She may choose to take time off during the nine months only for medical appointments and to deliver the baby. She may want several months off after the birth for herself and her newborn. Or, she may choose to stay at home for several years before going back into a full-tilt career at some point in time after the child enters school. In any case, some career disruption will occur.

Some women may take another tack—establish a family first, then enter the sales profession after the children are older and not as demanding of her time. Top revenue-producing females may be

[21] "Generation & Gender in the Workplace," *American Business Collaboration*, Families and Work Institute, Watertown, MA, 2004, 10, http://www.familiesandwork.org/announce/2002NSCW.html.

reluctant to pursue a promotion given the sacrifices they will have to make at home. The independent sales performer role gives a woman more flexibility than a sales management role might. As a sales rep, she can design her own schedule and travel, but as a manager, others often call the shots. She is also always on call when a client or team crisis erupts.

As a result of trying to resolve the "now or later" dilemma, many couples may put family—either having children or spending time with a spouse—on hold until a "better, more convenient time." For some, that convenient time never comes or it becomes more difficult, as evidenced by the growing fertility industry.

On the Road Again

A crucial lifestyle choice for female sales leaders is how much time to spend on the road, away from their husbands and children. One common rationale for offering executive level jobs to men rather than women is that it is easier for men to travel out of town than for women, who have the assumed added responsibility of caring for any children in the family.

Travel becomes a necessary part of the chief sales executive's job, our women respondents stated repeatedly. They must be on the front line to hire, train, grow and develop good salespeople and future leaders, as well as monitor and maintain client relationships. Chief sales executives must be available to join their teams or customers anywhere in the country, or even globally, and they no longer fully control their travel schedule. The corollary: they no longer control their family life schedule.

"Let's face it," explains Stacey Reid, vice president of sales, Chantal Corp. "I have three sons, an understanding husband and a full-time nanny, but I still have 85 percent of the responsibility for my family. My first priority has to be to prepare my sons to be good men. I can't do that and be on the road all the time. I have refused to take promotions because of the travel. I knew I couldn't balance work and home and be on the road. And a chief sales executive who is not in front of her customers and her reps is not able to sell. Anything my employer can do to make my job more virtual will pay off for both of us."

The sales profession itself is synonymous with constant travel, but sales leadership brings the added requirement of even more time on the road. Both male and female candidates often face the same choice: remain a salesperson with high commissions and control your schedule, or become a chief sales executive with more travel and increased responsibility, but perhaps less compensation.

The choices revolve around passion and lifestyle. "As a sales leader, one of my biggest thrills and responsibilities is to take 'lumps of clay' and mold them into successful salespeople that I can then send on down the career road," says Mary Delaney. "If that desire isn't a passion in the salesperson I am interviewing, I know that person won't be happy about the traveling lifestyle of a sales leader."

What if travel is not a fit? Delaney sees warning signs in individuals of either sex without even asking the question. "I once interviewed a sales manager for a next-level management position and asked him what he loved most about sales. He told me about his baby son, how one of the joys of his life was being there each evening to hold him before putting him to bed. He said, 'I love the control I have over my life. I know the rules and how to play the game. I perform, and my wife and I get to live in this great house and drive nice cars.' Right away, I knew this man loved sales but probably wouldn't love being a sales leader earning less and traveling more.

"When hiring a sales leader, especially if it would require moving to a different locale for the candidate, I bring in the whole family," Delaney says. "I take the couple to dinner and we talk about the role, the move, and what it might mean to the other spouse. I have seen it take a year for that second person to find the right job. That person has to know we understand and value his or her part in the new job and the move."

The 24/7 Factor

The changes that create new choices also blur the lines between professional and personal lives. For example, with the growing pressures of global competition, CEOs expect their head of sales to remain available 24/7 to close a key deal.

The female chief sales executives in our study say they meet that expectation because sales has been in their blood since they began their careers. Early on, these few successful women made a huge lifestyle decision—whether or not to have children, and if so, when and how to juggle that growing family and a thriving career simultaneously. By this point in their career, these women are fully aware of the time commitments

I Always Knew

COLLEEN HONAN
Senior Vice President, Global Sales, Services and Solutions
OneSource Information Services, Inc.

Honan knew at age 10 that she would be in sales. "I can remember meeting my dad at the door and asking him how his sales calls had gone that day. I was so social that sales and what he did fascinated me. I just always knew I wanted to sell."

Honan's passion is almost genetic. Her grandfather was also a salesperson whom she admired.

and are willing to be on call as needed. It was a conscious decision in their past to follow their passion for sales despite the obstacles, and they are focused and flourishing. Importantly, their life partners understand and cooperate with the inevitable family disruptions that the quick "Clark Kent to Superman" changes often require. However, even with the changing dynamics and increase in senior-level opportunities for females, many women still choose not to give up family and personal time, opting instead to wave goodbye to potential career advancement.

It all comes down to choices which often contradict accepted myths about women executives. Society perceives the successful top saleswoman as forceful, controlling and commanding in all facets of her life, at home and at work. For years, popular entertainment has cast the career woman as a merciless, take-charge executive with a wrecked home life. In the recent film, "The Devil Wears Prada," the character Miranda Priestly carries this image to the extreme.

The usual scenario around which family lifestyle decisions are made is the presence of young children. Who will be there to take cupcakes to school birthday parties, or to pick the children up from school when they are sick or to transport them to sports or dancing activities?

"When I had a small son at home, my boss helped me define a flexible consulting role to meet both my needs and the company's needs. I reported to the CEO and had the opportunity to restructure sales and marketing, as well as act as the vice president of sales part-time. It was a win-win," recalls Mary Delaney.

As inherent nurturers, women chief sales executives say they recognize the critical role that parents, teachers, mentors and coaches play in preparing the next generation to succeed. After all, someone must make it a priority to raise healthy children to become future workers and leaders. Either the father or mother must step up to the plate and take on the majority of this responsibility, which usually means the other parent steps further into the family outfield by immersing him or herself in the work environment as the main provider. While tradition says it is the woman's job to raise the children, perhaps the real question is whether both parents should share equally in that responsibility so that both can enjoy parental roles plus career success. Equality in these choices will not always be the same for every couple. It may involve an equal division of labor between childcare and employment for both parents at the same time, or it may be that one partner is the total caregiver for a set period of time and then the roles are reversed as the second partner pursues a career.

Whatever the decision, flexibility and adaptability are crucial attributes for the entire hierarchy of the work force—from entry-level recent graduates to the CEO, and the life partners who support these employees in their career climb. In fact, the true beneficiaries will be the children, who will have male and female role models on both sides of the work/childcare continuum.

Despite the stereotypical celluloid image, most of the women interviewed for this study found ways to succeed both at work and with family—and they made it to the top. Strong female leaders do indeed use their inherent nurturing and multi-tasking strengths by taking time to have successful marriages or partners, to raise families, to care for aging parents, and, as we will explore in a later chapter, even to take on the additional mantle of mentoring the next generation of women executives.

CHAPTER 5

Baby Boomers Engaging Millennials

Workers born between 1946 and 1964 drove the extraordinary growth of the U.S. economy over the past 50 years. Now in their mid-40s to mid-60s, these individuals entered the world during a large spike in the nation's birth rate following World War II. Referred to as Baby Boomers, this group numbers about 80 million and comprises about a quarter of the country's population. More than one-half are women.[22]

By the time they reach the C-suite, Baby Boomer female executives have already blown out the candles on their 40th or 50th birthday cakes and carved a path through the business wilderness. They have survived the hard battles of gender bias, made the tough choices about work and family and, along the way, honed their business skills to exceptional sharpness.

More affluent and healthier than previous generations, these women now find themselves on the brink of retiring from traditional

---

[22] Percentage of women baby boomers in 2005, http://www.census.gov/popest/national/.

workplace roles.[23] Despite the findings of a 2004 AARP study that 79 percent of the Baby Boomer generation planned to continue working in some fashion for several years rather than retire completely, this group already had begun to retire from traditional roles.[24] Many of them were anticipating several years of leisure and the chance to pursue activities they had no time for while holding down a full-time job. However, by the end of 2008, one in four Baby Boomers was rethinking retirement plans due to the economy. More women (31%) than men (19%) said they are changing their retirement plans—working longer than previously anticipated for income, health insurance and to build up their Social Security check amounts.[25] Even though delaying retirement may postpone the brain drain of the Baby Boomer generation, the question remains—who will fill their high-heels? Waiting in the wings, the Millennials discussed in Chapter 2 are eager to pursue careers and make their marks.

That pending wave of exiting Baby Boomers presents a problem, however, especially among the female business community. Every veteran female executive who retires from the workplace takes away rare and valuable attributes that Millennial workers want and need in order to succeed—knowledge, wisdom, perspective, support and counsel—all attained through sacrifice and hard work.

---

[23] Wan He, Manisha Sengupta, Victoria A. Velkoff and Kimberly A. DeBarros, "65+ in the United States: 2005," for the National Institute on Aging, U.S. Census Bureau.

[24] RoperASW, "Baby Boomers Envision Retirement II - Key Findings, Survey of Baby Boomers' Expectations for Retirement," prepared for AARP, copyright 2004, AARP, Knowledge Management, 601 E. Street, NW, Washington, DC 20049, 6, http://research.aarp.org.

[25] "Baby Boomers Are Changing Their Retirement Plans," http://www.usnews.com/blogs/planning-to-retire/2009/3/12/baby-boomers-are-changing-their-retirement-plans.html?s_cid=rss:planning-to-retire:baby-boomers-are-changing-their-retirement-plans.

Generational Motivators

MICHELE SARKISIAN
Sales Group Vice President
Maritz Inc.

Sarkisian is clear that she chose sales for the money. Yet she understands the way to motivate others may be different. Her team has had relatively little turnover—a result of her day-to-day mentoring of individuals and her willingness to work shoulder-to-shoulder with them. Sarkisian believes that sales is not about products, but relationships, and that women are more likely to take the time to develop those relationships and to invest in people—a philosophy that team-oriented Millennials eagerly endorse. Part of investing in people is providing time off for renewal and rejuvenation. Sarkisian says, "Baby Boomers look at maternity leave the way Millennials look at spiritual time off—different strokes for different folks." She understands that no matter what each individual does with his or her time away from the office, Millennials value periodic extended breaks from the work routine and will demonstrate increased productivity when they return to the job.

Sarkisian's training budget further reflects her commitment to the importance of off-site training (company-subsidized time off) to the attitude and efficiency of her staff. The workers of the younger generation, even more so than their predecessors, want to see their supervisors demonstrating that the company offers a wealth of opportunities for growth and advancement. If not, they will look elsewhere, taking their ideas and capabilities with them.

Well before they retire, can these successful Baby Boomer women use their natural ability to engage and guide up-and-coming 20-somethings? Are these women ready to share their experiences and hard-won wisdom? Will they be heard and be perceived as relevant to the younger generation?

All indications point to "Yes." Unlike prior generations, Millennials seem to relate to experienced leaders. Gone is belief in the 1960s' mantra that you cannot trust anyone over 30 years old. Millennials seem more independent-minded and objective, and are exhibiting a generational swing back toward traditional family values.[26] For these reasons, women are uniquely qualified to usher in this new generation of sales professionals.

---

[26] Mary Stamp, "Students Today Accept Traditional Beliefs," *The Fig Tree*, Washington State University, March 3, 2006, http://www.thefigtree.org/march06/stearns.html.

Not So Fast, Millennials

There is a bridge connecting the Baby Boomers and the Millennials. The path between the two has been paved by the Generation X, a smaller, less vocal and largely unsung generation. Generation X, also known as the Baby Buster generation, generally refers to those born from 1965 through the early 1980s. This generation experienced the fall of the Soviet Union and the emergence of the U.S. as the world's superpower. Unlike the next generation, as 20-somethings entering the work force just ahead of the Millennials, this group scornfully rejected the habits and values of the Baby Boomers, viewing that group as self-centered, fickle and impractical. Generation X children grew up in a time of increased drug use, elevated divorce rates and economic strain. These youth felt paralyzed by the social problems they saw as their inheritance—racial strife, homelessness, AIDS, fractured families and federal deficits.[27]

Ironically, one of the leading authors on Generation X, Douglas Coupland, objects to any stereotyping of this generation, saying that his book, *Generation X: Tales for an Accelerated Culture*, was intended to show the lack of a common set of traits for this generation.[28] All the same, this generation is generally characterized by its lack of optimism for the future, disenchantment, cynicism against the traditional values of the Baby Boomer generation, alienation and skepticism. Generation Xers often accuse the Baby Boomers of being hypocritical and greedy. In return, Baby Boomers often refer to the Generation Xers as lazy slackers. Generation Xers, approximately 48 million in the U.S., number just slightly more than half the Baby Boomer generation.

---

[27] Dan Cray, Tom Curry, and William McWhirter, "Twentysomething," *Time*, July 16, 1990.

[28] Douglas Coupland, *Generation X: Tales for an Accelerated Culture*, St. Martin's Press, New York, NY, 1991.

Yet, even as this generation has rebelled, somewhat overshadowed by their much larger sibling generation, the Millennials, Generation Xers have paved the way for the younger set to build careers in a more peaceful manner. In fact, it was perhaps the dissidence of the Generation Xers that caused the Baby Boomers to recognize, respect and appreciate the value of younger minds and different ways. After all, the pioneer generation always takes the arrows and little of the glory, but the baton of leadership must eventually and inevitably be passed.

Enter, Millennials

Millennial workers are those born between approximately 1978 and 2000. They number about 76 million, almost equal to the number of Baby Boomers. They view the world through the Internet, instant messages, video games, cell phones and blogs. Compared to Baby Boomers, these younger workers share fewer common viewing or listening experiences, thanks to iPods, social networks and the sheer number of media options that decentralize messages. Immigration and race relations in a global economy rank as their primary social issues.[29] Generally, Millennials accept multiculturalism and internationalism as the norm. They advocate the concepts of teams and organized sports. Their friends are many and diverse, as are their core beliefs.

Nell Howe and William Strauss, in *"Millennials Rising: The Next Great Generation,"* see this generation as one that willingly embraces law and order, collaboration, teamwork, morality, diversity and problem-solving. They predict that this generation "will recast

---

[29] Neil Howe and William Strauss, *Millennials Rising: The Next Great Generation*, Vintage Books, New York, NY, 2000.

the image of youth from downbeat and alienated to upbeat and engaged, with potentially seismic consequences for America."[30]

To Each His Own

In an insightful piece of research reported in the July 2007 *Harvard Business Review*, Howe and Strauss defined the key to understanding the Millennial generation's behaviors. "To learn why they (or any two generations) are different, one can look at how they were raised as children, what public events they witnessed in adolescence, and what social mission they took on as they came of age." The authors point out that because generations follow observable historical patterns, those patterns offer a powerful tool for predicting future trends and behaviors. "To anticipate what 40-year-olds will be like 20 years from now, don't look at today's 40-year-olds; look at today's 20-year-olds."[31] This predictor of Millennials as 40-year-olds may be one reason why Millennials are more open to learning from their Baby Boomer bosses. Whether either generation is cognizant of it or not, the similarities in core values and pivotal world events may be a key ingredient in their mutual respect.

Can We Relate?

How can a Baby Boomer female sales executive connect with this sea of eager young sales reps? The topic begs several questions.

First, does the Millennial generation even want advice from their Baby Boomer elders? Howe and Strauss state that old Baby Boomers'

---

[30] Howe and Strauss. *Millennials Rising.*

[31] Neil Howe and William Strauss, "The Next 20 Years: How Customer and Workforce Attitudes Will Evolve," *Harvard Business Review*, July-August 2007.

ethical perfectionism and "other-worldliness" will appear hypocritical and even eccentric to the younger generation. Yet, they believe Millennials may respect Baby Boomers for their vision and values, many of which they share.[32]

The cover article of a recent issue of *Fortune* illustrates Millennials' willingness, and even strong desire, to listen to the older generation. The article showcased young adults who want their parents' help in finding that all-important first job. "I was with my daughter for her first day at school," a woman is quoted in the article. "I was with her for her first day at college and I am here for her first day on the job."[33] Rather than a sign of insecure dependence, this dynamic more importantly signals that youths value the knowledge, wisdom and guidance of their elders.

Second, if the younger generation is willing to listen to Baby Boomers, how will the two generations effectively communicate? This is not a generation that wants to be told the answers. Kelly Koster and Alexandra Smith of Iconoculture remind us in a report on their blog that this is the Montessori generation—bred to believe that everyone is special and thus deserves a say, making them strong team players where every team member has just as much right to speak up as another.[34] Translated, that means that an entry-level sales rep is likely to pipe up during a meeting with a strategy idea with just as much self-perceived authority as the vice president of sales. After all, two bright heads are better than one, boss or not, right?

---

[32] Howe and Strauss, "The Next 20 Years," 48.

[33] Nadira A. Hira, "Attracting the Twentysomething Worker," *Fortune*, May 28, 2007.

[34] Kelly Koster and Alexandra Smith, "From Workplace to Marketplace: How Millennial work values translate into brand opportunity," Inconoculture, July 2007 blog.

Women chief sales executives can play a strong role in coaching Millennial women to develop their people and influencing skills, to understand internal and external organization dynamics, to "play the politics" and to grow the company. The executives will need to help their teams set objectives to groom the next generation of sales leaders while focusing younger workers on learning the ropes, as well as bringing fresh perspectives to the team.

Millennials Rising

Many Millennial youngsters, like the previous Generation X, grew up parentless, either due to divorce or virtually orphaned by Mom's and Dad's focus on building careers. As a result, they look for someone to take a stand and to speak hard truth to them. They want respected elders to confront them on choices and priorities. They want someone to set clear performance expectations and boundaries they may never have had, yet for which they have yearned. Boundaries mean someone is watching, and more importantly, caring. These young adults do not want their elders to be friends or bosses in title alone. They want to know their leaders are real and genuine even when those leaders have not performed up to perceived expectations.[35] They want to draw upon the strengths that women leaders seem to have in abundance—support and nurturing.

Members of this young generation also seek something new, some action they can take to make a difference. Indeed, they have the talent and ability to do great things. But pride and a subtle bitterness often get between Baby Boomers and Millennials. "We need each other,"

---

[35] Lisa Borden, "Next Gen Wants You," *Discipleship Journal,* NavPress®, May/June 2007:159, 46.

says one Millennial in a recent *Discipleship Journal* article. "When we go off on our own, we put ourselves in a dangerous place."[36]

In fact, according to Howe and Strauss, Millennial youths may be expected to rebel against their parents' Baby Boomer narcissism, impatience and argumentative bent by acting instead of talking.[37] They are already involved in volunteerism at record levels, showing a willingness to try to make the world a better place against the odds. Indeed, many colleges and universities now consider an applicant's record of community service as a factor in the admission process.

Will these young people heed the career advice of a chief sales executive who is the age of their mother? Perhaps the saving grace will be in the old adage that an expert is someone who lives 50 miles or more away, or at least outside one's own home! A young woman may not listen to Mom, but she may listen to someone else's mom bearing the credentials of an important title and a powerful brand.

Why Not Have a Life?

As Millennials grow into leadership roles, the once-traditional holistic female role may become the norm. Already, they are asking, "Why not live a life that includes family, fun, work and service to humanity? Why not be there for career day at my child's school, sports activities, family travel or volunteer opportunities? Long before multi-tasking, flexibility, and work-life balance became the norm, women were struggling to keep ahead both at home and at the office, often with little support at either venue.

---

[36] Borden, 46.

[37] Howe and Strauss, "The Next 20 Years."

Millennials provide a contrast to female Baby Boomers, who faced roadblocks, became off-ramped from careers or downsized their ambitions. The employees of this newer generation express no need for on- and off-ramping, and see no stigma in taking time off or working flextime, actions that the older generation would equate to being a "loser," or at best, less ambitious. *Indeed, Millennials often demand workplace changes as part of their due, whereas Baby Boomer women have spent decades chipping away at the walls surrounding corporate change.*

Time will tell if change occurs, as Baby Boomers help these youths climb the corporate ladders and assume leadership positions in society.

CHAPTER 6

The Road Ahead

Life in the work world is about to change, and generational differences are only a part of that dichotomy.

That should be no surprise, because the human and natural worlds remain in constant flux—they always have been and always will be. In our human world of work, we see continual shifting in opportunities, lifestyles, demographics and traditions.

As female executives tread water in this sea of change, two issues keep bobbing up to the surface and demanding attention. The first issue is all about doing the right thing, not only personally in aspiring to achieve meaningful lives, but also for generations to follow. The recent, heightened interest in protecting the environment for the future stands as one example of how Americans now more consciously consider the anticipated needs of those yet unborn as they make decisions to meet the immediate needs of today's generation. Similarly, choices each individual makes about his or her personal work life (career path, salary, location, office environment, expertise and influence) are analogous to pebbles tossed into a pond. The ripples travel outward from the center, affecting families, social contacts and descendents, in unknown yet broadening patterns. The residual ripples of one person's choices mingle with those of spouses and associates to create complex dynamics that are the foundation of daily living.

The second issue, the rate of change, looms large and no one ever seems satisfied. Changes come either too rapidly or too slowly, depending upon individual needs and orientation. The Constitutional change allowing women to vote, for example, came at a snail's pace for most females, but startled many men with the cheetah-like speed of its arrival. The analogy carries over into the world of work, where changes in practices, policies, technology, culture and leadership styles occur surprisingly quickly at some companies while seeming to merely plod along at others.

The increasing emphasis on business innovation, constant demographic shifts and the need to groom the next generation all portend enormous opportunities for aspiring female leaders to reach their full potential on the road ahead. But how do they position themselves to garner the most advantage from these opportunities?

Waves of Innovation

If need is the father of invention, then desire is the mother of innovation, especially in the corporate arena.

Hand-in-hand, invention and innovation historically displace existing products, services and methodologies with more effective and efficient solutions. As our American culture progressed, factories wiped out blacksmith shops, automobiles doomed the horse and buggy makers and corporations overwhelmed individual proprietorships.[38] To make

---

[38] Thomas McCraw, *Prophet of Innovation: Joseph Schumpeter and Creative Destruction*, Belknap Press of Harvard University Press, 2007.

a change required courage, and with every change came some pain. That scenario continues at an even faster pace today.

Inviting more females into executive ranks stands out as such an innovation. Driven by the desire to do what is best for the company, a courageous CEO may step beyond the comfort zone and hire a qualified female for a traditionally male position. Just as important as new products, innovative approaches to utilizing and promoting people from within keeps an organization ahead of competition. When it comes to finding and retaining top talent, the first to the table chooses from the cream of the crop. The historically overlooked cream is often a female.

"When I interviewed with MSA in the early 1980s, I think they saw my talent, because they brought me in as their first female sales rep in the country," Deb Gallagher of Pinnacle Selling recalls. "To see if I could do the job, they placed me in the North and South Dakota territories. Well, in my first territory, I became the number one rep. Then I was made district manager and given the worst performing district of all 22 districts in the company. In two years, I took that district from last place to number one. In 1984 in Los Angeles, when I was promoted to western regional manager, that region was also the worst performing out of 11 regions. Again, we took it to number one. Once I proved myself, I was given every opportunity to advance that a man would have been given."

A key point to grasp is that early innovators gain competitive advantage, and this holds true in the selection of leaders, as well as in general business issues. The earlier the innovation occurs, the greater the value of that innovation. For example, a company gains great value by hiring its first female sales leader. Hiring a woman to a top sales slot gets the attention of customers. It shows a commitment to change, diversity and differentiation. Indeed, presenting a woman in such a visible executive role may provide the company with competitive advantage in its marketplace. Hiring the 10th female leader will be less of an innovation, and hiring the 500th will be merely commonplace.

Senior managers who choose to place organizational success above personal success will acquire the best female sales leaders for their company because they will have the option of choosing from a large and motivated talent pool of super-qualified candidates who love what they do, do it well, and are eager to prove their ability to bring value to the company. In a dynamic labor market, demand will grow substantially as more female sales leaders demonstrate their abilities and their impact on the bottom line. Thus, CEOs who place women in top positions later rather than sooner will do so at far less risk (others having paved the way), but with fewer choices for top talent (the super-qualified having already been promoted or lured away to greener pastures).

The Millennial Tsunami

While innovation relates to "how" things change, a much broader shift looms over the horizon—"who" is changing. The answer is: our work force. The Baby Boomer generation will begin to retire in large numbers around 2011. These workers will be replaced with an ironically almost equal number of incoming workers from the Millennial demographic.[39] Our research suggests that females tend to be highly effective managers of this young age group—a group of workers who are socially aware, technologically savvy and individuality

---

[39] Dana French, "The Boomers' Kids, Generation Y, Are Poised to Take the Reins," *Casual Living*, April 1, 2006.

Career Management

Senior Global Sales Executive
Large Public IT Firm

This chief sales executive says she never consciously managed her career. Yet, her counsel on career development is sought by men and women alike. "I tell my colleagues not to use me as an example because as an engineer, I love a challenge. I love fixing a broken thing, so no one of my experiences seems like the logical step to the next experience." She thinks many women who might be very good at sales have never considered sales as a profession because "they haven't been around sales and don't really get sales, so they automatically think they would not be very good at it."

She advises young people to gain as many different job experiences as possible to build skills. She says that being in a large corporation has enabled her to move from one brand to another, one product line to another, one industry sector to another and one geographical location to another without leaving the company. Each move has helped her enhance the broader portfolio of sales leadership skills needed to keep advancing her career inside her company.

driven. The first wave of this new breed of employee, an estimated 35 million of which are women, has already graduated from college and begun entering the lower echelons of industries across the country.[40] Managers of Millennials must lead with a style that respects these qualities or risk losing the new talent to competitors who are more attuned to the differing values between established employees and the fledgling workers.

Although the workplace will soon be awash in these Millennial employees, most female salespeople today fall within Generation X, positioned in between the Baby Boomers and the Millennials. This places Generation X women in a unique role as the conduits to transfer knowledge to the younger generation. In Chapter 12, we delve further into this phenomenon.

Aside from the chaotic social era these youth grew up in, there were other forces contributing

---

[40] 2006 U.S. Department of Labor, *2006 Annual Averages*, 2007 Center for Women's Business Research, (accessed October 10, 2007).

to the Generation Xer's status as a sort of bridge between the Baby Boomers and the Millennials.[41] The significantly smaller size of this generation, approximately half of the generation on either side of them, hints at a critical cultural shift. The drop in the number of Generation X children born to the Baby Boomers reflects the change in manner in which progeny have been viewed by society over the past few decades. In the early part of the 20th century, as the U.S. economy began the transition from a rural, agrarian base to a more urbanized and industrial economic foundation, having a large number of children at home was no longer a necessity. They were not needed to help run the farm on a daily basis to sustain the family as in the past. Therefore, an increasing number of children became factory workers until child labor reforms outlawed using children to toil in factories or other commercial enterprises.

As these post-war, Baby Boomer children benefited from fewer family responsibilities and the urbanization of the U.S., their educational opportunities increased dramatically, thereby opening doors to job prospects and financial success that their parents and grandparents had never imagined possible. As the opportunities for these Generation Xers increased, so did their consciousness of the social obligations and financial costs of raising a healthy and community-oriented child from infancy to adulthood. Their Baby Boomer parents' drive for financial success and desire for each of their children to "have it all" are key factors in the decrease in the Generation X birth rate. Baby Boomer couples began to produce fewer children than previous generations and lavished more time and money on each. The Generation Xers had multiple opportunities and extravagant allowances thrust upon them,

---

[41] Linda Gravett, Ph.D, SPHR, "Building a Bridge Across Generations," e-HResources.com, http://www. e-hresources.com/Articles/Sept1.htm.

probably more than they could adequately embrace. So although they are more conscious of and involved in their role in society, it is perhaps this profusion of wealth and activities in their formative years that bred the attitude of entitlement for which this generation is often berated.

The decline in the birth rate not only changed a generation's composite attitude, but also created a new family dynamic. As a direct result of the increase in education and income levels over the past 50 years or so, many more women are choosing to remain completely childless, which was unheard of just a few generations ago. A woman only remained childless if she was physically unable to bear a child. The variety of birth control methods and the change in the way children are viewed within the context of the total family have allowed women to consciously plan their adult life. Marriage, then baby, then career? Career, then baby? One baby, then career, then another baby? The choices are hers. According to U.S. Census data of all U.S. women, in 1976, 36 percent had four or more children, and only 9 percent had one child. By 2001, the number of women with only one child had doubled to 18 percent, while the total of women with four or more children had dropped steeply to less than 10 percent.[42]

The mothers in the latter statistic above are Generation X women. They saw what their Baby Boomer mothers had initiated by attempting to combine family and career in ways that enabled them to be successful at both. The Generation Xers have taken that concept to the next level by choosing to have fewer children, carefully timing the birth of those children, and positioning themselves to be visible and effective in their careers as they concurrently rear those children. The Millennial generation of women is now nipping at the heels of

---

[42] Stephanie Mencimer, "The Baby Boycott – decline in birth rates attributed in part to Family Leave Act," *The Washington Monthly*, June 2001.

the Generation Xers—droves of determined and focused females are in entry-level positions in industries throughout the U.S. armed with even more carefully calculated and organized life plans in terms of career vs. family.

Progressive CEOs must realize that for all their non-traditional profiles, Generation Xers and Millennials represent the future leadership of the country's companies, and more of these leaders will be women than ever before. While the number of executives currently remains lopsided in favor of males, some trends project slightly upward for women. The Business and Professional Women's Foundation estimates that females will hold 27 percent of all corporate officer positions (up from 16 percent currently) by year 2020. Additionally, the Foundation reports that the wage gap between men and women, which narrows slightly each year, may finally disappear in another 30 years.[43]

The women sales leaders of Generation X who built their careers on the knowledge and foundation that their pioneering Baby Boomer predecessors established must stay attuned to the varied needs and learning styles of the Millennials and be proactive in their support of these neophytes. The road ahead remains fraught with obstacles as females in sales continue the struggle to dispel firmly entrenched and outdated ideas about women's roles in the hierarchy of an organization. Substantial chinks have been carved out of the traditional sales pyramid, but more solid planks must be inserted via demonstrated management competency by large numbers of women in order to boost competent females to the pinnacle of the male-dominated structure that continues to exist in too many organizations.

---

[43] "101 Facts on the Status of Workingwomen," 1.

Section Two

THE FEMALE STRENGTHS

CHAPTER 7

Finding Strengths

As in any leadership position, the chief sales executive must possess certain strengths first to achieve the position, and then to succeed and grow in it. Women who aspire to the top job must convince the higher-ups that they are strong enough for the task. To do so means overcoming entrenched perceptions about the strength of women, both physical and mental. Right off the bat, women must confront the notion of the "weaker sex," a misleading label whose origins seem to be tied to the narrow attributes of physical size and lifting power—men being, on average, taller and more muscular than women. Coupling this female dearth of physical strength with an equal lack of mental prowess is a mistake that many senior executives make, albeit perhaps not even consciously. But power does not just mean how much an individual can bench press—the whole concept of selling is based on an altogether different kind of power—the power to convince and persuade. Mental acuity, superb verbal skills and the ability to exhibit appropriate non-verbal cues to the client are strengths that are critical to sales.

Hmmmm. Now which gender is it that our society recognizes as the undisputed "top dog" in these critical areas? It is women who possess the real power in these vital sales strengths. Unfortunately, getting past the initial stigma of being the weaker sex has to come first before the female salesperson can actually prove that she can be a successful leader. The author's mantra has always been, "Make them so impressed with your brains that they forget you have breasts, or at least only notice each in that order."

Ironically, women have been disproving the weaker sex concept for millennia. Our earliest female ancestors may not have been the powerful wild game hunters, but they were strong enough to bear children and protect their families while farming, gathering, and providing for them, and smart enough to run the family and community while the men were away hunting for months on end. How did that ever become known as the weaker sex?

In more recent times, Rosie the Riveter and her generation did the same for the four long years of war that took the men of our country far from home and hearth. Even as recently as the 2008 U.S. presidential elections, women were contenders for the top two positions in the

Perfect Combination

STACEY REID
Vice President, Sales
Chantal Corp.

Reid grew up with a father and grandfather who were traveling salesmen. She became known as a tomboy because she loved all the things her father, older brother and grandfather enjoyed—sports, cars and athletics. She said it was only later that she realized her tomboy hobbies, combined with her trim figure and feminine good looks, were the perfect combination for a saleswoman.

There is a downside, Reid notes. "It can be a double-edged sword to be both. One moment you are cool and the next you are an aggressive bitch."

country—a grueling process involving the most intense selling possible. Yet, regardless of the credentials of the two or their track records as leaders, many men and women alike first judged their candidacy in terms of gender. It seems the stereotype of the inadequate female sex is still alive and well despite women having repeatedly demonstrated their ability to do "men's work" in leadership, hard work and sales. Clearly, women have more work to do to dispel the notion of being the weaker sex.

When competing against men for top jobs in the business world, a woman needs to demonstrate many strengths other than physical—intelligence, character, mental and emotional stamina, persistence and patience, to name a few. To stand out in the often male crowd, a woman must first recognize and embrace her inherent strong traits, build on those, then develop others as needed.

"We are attracted to the leadership quality of people who know their strengths and can articulate those strengths easily and comfortably," observes Cathy Perry, CEO and founder, InwardBound Coaching. "Let's say I could choose which of two women vice presidents I would work for," she poses. "One of them is comfortable in her role and speaks with pride about her accomplishments, her team and herself. The other woman is wishy-washy and self-effacing—not an advocate. For whom do I want to work? Number one. It is totally magnetic to be around people who own their strengths."

Naturally, each of us develops strengths and abilities thanks to our genetic makeup and to environmental forces that influence our growth from day one. Our genes represent the cards we are dealt for physical features, talents, intelligence and other innate traits. We may want to alter our genetic code from time to time (an extra three inches in height would have been nice, thank you), but we must all utilize the strengths of the design we have been given.

Environmental factors, on the other hand, affect *how* we play our gene cards. Influences ranging from living conditions to subcultures greatly affect our career direction and rate of development. Yet, our most powerful environmental force very well may be the role models we meet along the way—people who help us aim high in life and actualize our inner strengths to get us there.

Business leaders, bosses, parents, teachers, peers, coaches and others all help to shape—for better or worse—our character, values, attitudes and passions that last a lifetime.

Business Leaders

Males typically have available a wide range of success-directed role models, from whom they observe and internalize concepts such as winning, discipline, reaching for the top, being stronger than the opposition, and succeeding. In business, many more males than females occupy top positions and thereby serve as de facto role models to others. As a result, men often experience confidence-boosting success early in their careers. The top spot seems attainable, and they are encouraged to go for it. Females, in contrast, find fewer high-level role models in the competitive business world, and certainly less encouragement.

Many of the women we interviewed benefited from strong influences in the home—powerful parents instilling in these exceptional women from an early age that anything is possible. However, most found few clear role models outside of the home to emulate as they moved into the working world and strove to define themselves as strong, directed, success-oriented professionals.

Ellen Cook, in an article in Career Development Quarterly, suggests that women consciously or subconsciously seek out other women to tell them what is appropriate and possible, including roles to pursue as careers. To prepare for careers in business and other professions, therefore, women must reach into those professions for guidance, inspiration and, most importantly, development of their innate strengths. For women seeking top sales management positions, helpful role models tend to be people who successfully combine work and family obligations. Given the variety of obstacles these women are likely to face along the path to the top, they learn much from both genders and from individuals encompassing a variety of socio-economic backgrounds.[44] Because relatively few women head up sales organizations, however, women in this particular career track find few female role models. The female chief sales executives we talked with adamantly state their intention to fill this void for the next generation of young women climbing the sales management ladder today.

Judy Fick, vice president and general manager of worldwide sales for Unisys, learned from some of the best. She worked for former IBM chairman, Lou Gerstner, during the critical years of reshaping "Big Blue" to survive into the next generation. She also worked for Carly Fiorina during Fiorina's pivotal time as head of Hewlett Packard. Regardless of how history will record the efforts of either CEO, Fick learned first-hand from the top CEOs of their time and industry, the art of designing and executing change—largely through the sales function. Since Fick is known for turning around stagnant or sliding sales organizations, it appears that she learned her lesson well.

---

[44] Ellen P. Cook, Mary J. Heppner and Karen M. O'Brien, "Career development of women of color and White women: assumptions, conceptualization, and interventions from an ecological perspective - Special Section," *Career Development Quarterly*, June 2002.

Another woman sales executive, Jocelyn Talbot, vice president of sales for RetirementJobs.com and formerly senior vice president of sales for Monster.com, also found role models in male industry leaders. She had the opportunity to be hired and mentored by an industry icon, Andy McKelvey, former chairman of TMP Worldwide and later, by Monster.com president, Steve Pogorzelski. "Through eight years of rapid growth and chaos at Monster, it was tough, but exciting," Talbot recalls. "I learned a lot from Steve about how to build the sales organization in a rapid-growth company. Steve promoted me to vice president and then senior vice president—because I performed." She puts that compendium of knowledge to use in her current chief sales executive role.

The Boss

When asked what traits her ideal CEO would have, Stacey Reid, of Chantal Corp., said, "That person needs to be married, with children, to have a clue about what we go through as women with families."

Indeed, the CEO serves as perhaps the company's best model for what it takes to be successful in that organization, and the top sales position reports to the CEO. Since very few women are CEOs and men also fill most of the top sales slots, by default it is men who most often serve as role models for the current generation of sales women who aspire to the top sales job. Because of the prominence of their position, CEOs of both genders should be constantly aware that employees model their words and actions upon what the top leaders say and do—good or bad, right or wrong.

Two great women bosses influenced her along the way, recalls Colleen Honan, senior vice president of global sales, service and solutions for OneSource Information Services, Inc. After being passed over for promotion in favor of a less-qualified male, Honan joined another company. Her new boss, a woman, gave her an opportunity to learn the product in a client support role with a promise to then move her into sales. This boss proved true to her word, showing Honan the right way to encourage women to acquire the necessary skills to move up the ladder. Honan's boss's attitude is commendable and contrary to some in upper management, who do not follow through on promises after they have put time and resources into training an individual for a certain critical, but lower-level position. The frustration this causes may be a factor in the disheartening numbers of women who just give up and resign themselves to stagnating in the lower position.

Later in the same company, another woman boss believed so much in Honan that she split her own sales territory and gave half to Honan. That is confidence, indeed! Honan demonstrates what she learned from these women by continuing to recruit good women and men, then providing on-going developmental opportunities and mentoring. Once the neophytes are in the door, the time and energy-intensive job of nurturing them to the point of leadership has just begun.

Lisa Cutts, vice president of sales at Misys Healthcare, jumped from a programming job into sales because her boss offered her a marketing opportunity that he thought might be more challenging *and* allow her to make more money. "I had become so bored that I was considering going part-time. When he made me that offer, I went from considering part-time to working in over-drive and haven't stopped climbing up the sales ladder since."

Parents

As evidenced by the author's own childhood experience, parents play a powerful, formative role in a person's expectation of what he or she can achieve in life. The more any child observes competent adults of his or her same gender, race, social and economic status performing a variety of roles and tasks, the more likely the child is to assume that such options are open to anyone.

Over and again, without being asked the question, our interviewees confided that their fathers influenced them more than all others to choose sales as a business career. Hard-working mothers, often toiling at low-paying jobs, fueled their passion for becoming self-sufficient. In addition to these influences, if a girl observes her mother appropriately balancing home and career priorities, she will learn by emulating Mom. Of course, Dad's attitude toward Mom's career, as well as whether or not he shoulders an equal part of the home and childcare responsibilities, plays a pivotal role in how the children will view their own spousal or partner relationships in the future.

Michele Sarkisian, sales group vice president at Maritz Inc., adds that she was fortunate to grow up in a home where her parents conveyed

I Proved Myself

CORRINE PERRITANO
Executive Vice President - Direct to Consumer Business
Jenny Craig, Inc.

Perritano had no brothers to take over the family business when her father fell unexpectedly ill while she was in college, so she ended up running a thoroughbred horse farm.

"At first, the men didn't take me seriously because I was so young and a female in a male business. You had to know a lot of math and statistics to place horses in races and with the owners. Eventually, I proved myself. They realized I knew what I was doing and we worked well together."

Perritano was able to finish college later, but for her the winning combination was her first-hand experience and her real-life business education.

a "no-victim mentality." Just as many of the women we interviewed, Sarkisian felt that perhaps the most significant gift her parents had given her was the belief that there were no differences between men and women in terms of capability and potential. There should be no excuses.

As both parents influence a child's self-esteem and interests, parents often are the first line of defense to encourage girls to conquer the historically shunned math and science fields of study. Consider the potential impact when a mother tells her six-year-old daughter, "Math is too hard for girls, so don't worry if you can't do well in it," or, "You don't want to take that chemistry class, you're a girl and you'll do much better in English."

Teachers

As in technology and other fields, a key factor in success for sales leaders is proficiency in mathematics, often perceived as a male-oriented subject. Where does one begin to build a good foundation in math? At school, of course, where teachers serve as pivotal role models for both boys and girls.

Several years ago, before off-shoring and outsourcing were household words, labor gurus realized that there would soon be a shortage of engineering and information technology specialists if only boys chose to pursue careers in math and sciences. Girls Inc.'s national *Operation SMART* is an example of a program that was developed to take preventive steps to avoid the impending shortage.[45] The research

---

[45] Girls Inc. *Operation SMART* is an approach to engaging girls and young women in inquiry-based science, technology, engineering and math through hands-on, minds-on experiences. Developed by: Girls Incorporated* with funding from National Science Foundation, The Ford Foundation, The Carnegie Corporation of New York, The Coca Cola Foundation, CREW Foundation, General Motors Foundation, Verizon Communications, Lucent Technology Foundation, National Endowment for the Humanities, and many others.

behind *Operation SMART* found that if girls do not enjoy math and science by ages 6 to 13, they likely will not develop a comfort with numbers and technologies at any later point in life. That statistic helps to explain why even as recently as 2001, as the tail-end of the Generation Xers entered the work force, only 3 percent of college graduates in engineering and math were women.[46]

By limiting the scope of girls' skills, their job and career choices also are limited. That consequence is important, because employees in the generations from the Baby Boomers through the Millennials will likely not only move from job to job, but also from career to career many times during their work life. Gone are the days of hiring on in a company's stock room and retiring with that gold watch 40 or 50 years later.

Clearly, girls must be equipped to choose positions such as sales that require an understanding of numbers, or they will not even view these types of positions as viable options. Females must have early role models and equal access in the classroom to the materials, research and ideas that will open their minds to the possibilities of math- and science-oriented professions. A young woman will steer clear of even entry-level sales if she has no confidence in her mathematical abilities or has had no encouragement to strengthen a demonstrated aptitude for numbers in her formative years. The foundation for expanding already existing male-dominated programs exists, but is not being fully utilized.

In an on-point article published in *Computing Research News*, Senator Ron Wyden of Oregon discusses how the amendment passed

---

[46] *Postsecondary Education*, U.S. Department of Education, National Center for Education Statistics, 2002, http://nces.ed.gov/pubs2003/digest02/tables/dt278.asp.

in 1972 known as Title IX has substantially broadened and enhanced the rights of young women in a variety of sports, but the same parity has not yet been achieved in the classroom. Ironically, Senator Wyden asserts, the focus of the law was originally directed toward equality in *educational opportunities*, not sports. At the time the amendment was passed, the inequities of gender representation in the math, science and technology fields had become a national concern. Based on reports from various agencies over the years, "...America's failure to invest in science and to reform math and science education [is] the second biggest threat to our national security, greater than that from any conceivable conventional war." Wyden notes that encouraging girls and enhancing educational programs via Title IX is not only the right thing to do, but the smart thing to do.[48]

In making his case, Wyden also alludes to the cultural stereotypes that discourage young girls from showing an interest in math or science, and the lack of female role models in these areas, which subsequently leads to a lack of expectations for girls to achieve. However, as an example of the fact that these stereotypes can be overcome, he relates a story told to him by the president of a science and industry museum. Staffers of the museum noticed that many young girls walked into the museum thinking that science and math were for boys. In fact, when the girls were asked to draw pictures of a scientist, they all drew an older white man in a lab coat. However, after participating in enrichment programs at the museum, those same girls drew pictures of women in lab coats. They had begun to imagine themselves and their

---

[47] Senator Ron Wyden, "Title IX and Women in Academics," *Computing Research News*, September 2003, vol. 15, no.4, 1.

[48] Wyden, 8.

peers as mathematicians, scientists and engineers.[48]

To make a sustainable difference, the focus on encouraging more girls to embrace math and science must begin by providing qualified teachers in elementary school, then expanding the emphasis through junior high, high school and college. In addition, opportunities for girls to participate in extracurricular activities that require the practice and honing of these skills (chess club, science club, math competitions, rocketry seminars, etc.) must be presented in attractive and enticing ways, beginning during the upper elementary school years. Teachers continue to play a crucial role during these activities, as they are the ones in the supervisory roles and can encourage girls to participate and compete with their male counterparts—a role they will need to embrace during their future in the business world. An understanding and supportive teacher can play an important role in persuading a shy and awkward adolescent to step out of her comfort zone and participate in a group that consists mainly of boys—creatures that she and her friends view with a mixture of awe, fear and disgust.

Peers

With school years behind them, young women interested in sales begin to ascend the career ladder and peers become a source of continuous learning. These are people with whom the neophyte business woman competes, supports, critiques and engages on a daily basis. Sadly, however, women have few female peers from whom to learn.

Mary Delaney, of CareerBuilder.com, pointed out that in 1986 she was the only woman out of 312 attendees at Carnation's annual sales meeting. The peers she learned from were the men in the room, not because they were better, but because they were there.

Beth Doherty, vice president of sales for Emdigo, Inc., and formerly sales director at Sony, recalls taking a woman peer "on the road" with her to demonstrate, rather than tell her, what a typical day in Doherty's life was like. The woman reported that she "learned more spending that single day with Beth than she had in all her other training." This was obviously a powerful sales demonstration.

These women who had so few female peers from whom to learn have never forgotten how that felt. Many of them have taken special pains to encourage candidates with high potential, male and female, to become sales executives. They are especially thrilled to see women they have groomed become successful.

During telephone interviews with women executives, when we asked what makes them different from male peers, the pause often was so long we thought the line had dropped.

"Are you still there?" we would ask.

"Oh, yes," came the response. "It's just that there have not been many women executives to observe. Over time, you realize you are learning from your peers, but you just never differentiate men and women that way."

CHAPTER 8

Nurture Vs. Numbers

Studies abound regarding the male-female gender dynamic. A key conclusion of our own study of female chief sales executives indicates that men usually tune in to the logic of numbers to influence outcomes, whereas women tap into their emotional base to nurture those people who can improve results. Progressive organizations understand this reality and seek to utilize the innate and learned talents of both genders to best advantage. The secret lies in wisely matching those unique strengths to specific jobs. Clearly, a central issue in the business leadership arena is not male vs. female. The issue is numbers vs. nurturing, and it plays out in many ways.

How Many vs. How Well

Our study reveals a consistent, powerful contrast in how men and women relate to their business worlds; men place value on quantities, and women focus on helping people succeed.

For example, male chief sales executives can present compelling data in the boardroom, but they often remain distant from front-line personnel realities, many times with costly results. Female chief sales executives, however, tend to dive into people issues to reduce turnover and boost productivity, yet still must search for numbers that show how the business is doing.

When questioned about business data, nearly all the women chief sales executives in our study deferred the answer to another person, usually a male. Those females who did respond asked for more time to provide the numbers, either in writing or in a follow-up phone call. In addition, when asked to summarize their priorities for success, women respondents placed numbers far down on the list. More important than specific numbers, they said, are hiring the right people in the right roles, letting people know they make a difference, providing continuous feedback, communicating and involving their people in all aspects of their function and imbuing in them the overall mission. It is the people driving the results, not the figures themselves, that make a company successful.

Success Priorities

- Hiring the right people in the right roles

- Letting people know they make a difference

- Providing continuous feedback

- Communicating and involving people in all aspects of their function

- Imbuing people with the organization's mission

- Proficiency with numbers

One of our interviewees, the senior global sales executive at a major IT firm, leads the second highest revenue-contributing division at her company, with annual sales well into the billions of dollars. She believes that to manage a large sales force one must understand the art and science of both sales and leadership.

Listening to Learn, Not to Respond

REBECCA BERNSON
*Senior Vice President,
National Accounts Sales*
**Automatic Data Processing,
Inc. (ADP)**

Bernson climbed the sales ladder and stayed with the same company for 25 years before she chose to take the job at ADP. It was a huge decision for her. "I was a very long interview cycle. Most of our conversations were about relationships. I never asked for the job, like a good salesperson should. My future boss simply asked me, 'Is there reason for us to meet again?' at the end of each meeting. Eventually, I believed it was the right thing for me to make the move." Once on the job in her new company, Bernson continued to focus on relationships. "It was not a conscious thing, but looking back, it was all I could do. I truly needed their help and asked questions without any preconceived ideas about people, ideas or politics. I quickly built partnerships because people understood that I was listening to learn, not to respond."

By illustration, this executive points to a personal success—turning around an operating unit saddled by a history of poor performance. Sales metrics had been clearly established and just as clearly missed year after year. Although willing and able to manage the numbers side of the business, she chose instead to solve the root problems by developing her people. First step: instill in everyone the values and purpose of the organization. Why start with values? Because values drive people to perform toward the goals or performance metrics.

"Many people thought I was missing the point in the beginning, but I realized it wasn't the people who were broken," she relates. "They had just lost track of what is important in our organization and why they were here. When employees really understand the purpose of their job and believe they can make the business better—and when they know that their supervisors are watching out for them—they will do their best work and won't leave, even for higher salaries." Indeed, the executive confirms a recent finding by *FastCompany* magazine that people do not leave companies; they leave managers.[49] Her soft-skill approach is paying off in hard dollars. Three years after taking over the unit, 90 percent of the sales force remains on board, compared to a cross-industry average turnover of 39 percent during the same period.[50] Significantly, the salespeople in her division now meet every metric goal set before them—and in her words, "make a difference by being in the business."

Numbers Shy

Our observation in interviewing female chief sales executives— that they are less likely to know the numbers off the top of their heads than their male counterparts—appears particularly significant. Men generally seem to keep those numbers at their fingertips. At first, we thought our questions about numbers were unclear, such as how many activities it takes to convert a lead into a completed transaction. But it was not a lack of comprehension. These women simply could not spout off statistics that men apparently know and regularly use as bragging rights on the competitive field. The actual numbers were far less important to the women than was the overall success of the sales team.

Nor was it a lack of ability to know and talk numbers. They are smart women. Many of these women had math or science in their

---

[49] Clay Dillow, "Numerology: National Boss Day," *FastCompany*, copyright 2008 by Mansueto Ventures, LLC, ISSN 1085-9241, New York, NY, October 2008, no. 129, 42.

[50] Maureen Hrehocik, "The Best Sales Force: Finding, Keeping, Grooming," October 1, 2007, citing Greg Alexander, CEO of *Sales Benchmark Index*, in survey of 3,700 U.S. publicly traded companies across 19 industries from 1996-2006.

backgrounds. But in most every case, they needed to ask someone who "handled the numbers part" or "get back to us." The immediate and blunt reaction of the men participating on our interview team was, "She would never make it to the top in most organizations." Unfortunately, that is quite likely the reaction of more men than not in the real world work place. There is painful truth in the adage that perception is reality. Once the perception is created, it is a long and arduous path for a bright female sales executive to correct the damaging perception.

Here we begin to see *major differences* between the way men and women operate in sales management. Women seem to focus on the long-term relationship they have with their team members, as well as with their clients. Most women we interviewed felt that female chief sales executives are perfectly capable of conversing about numbers and certainly measure success by the same numerical scales as men, but prefer to focus on nurturing and teaching—personal investments which they see as key to building the skills of the people who deliver those numbers. They delegate the actual number crunching, storing and reporting to someone else. They seem to be saving their mind share for people relationship development.

An interesting case in point can be demonstrated by the quota-setting process. Both women and men comprehend what it takes to create a specific result. For example, if the goal this year is $2 billion in revenue, they must have 1,000 reps each selling $2 million. So, what must they have in the sales funnel in order to meet the target? How many calls does it take to get those dollars? Each gender attacks the challenge in a different manner. Men use the industry averages to extrapolate how much they can sell given their resources, even if that calculation exceeds the quota. Women work from the other direction.

Females seem to accept the overall quota target as given and then work the math to back into that number.

The larger concern, however, centers on how conversant the man or woman is about numbers when talking to the CEO, board members and stock analysts. For example, when asked for client acquisition costs, the male sales executive of a fast-growing software firm quickly summarized the figures, then cited each by lead source, comparing the effectiveness of direct mail, print advertising and paid search. Our observations indicate that his female counterparts would not lean toward that kind of detailed presentation of numbers. In this case, command of the numbers built confidence in those around the chief sales executive. A lack of command of those numbers has the opposite effect. Female chief sales executives would be wise to take note and master their numbers, as an added building block to support their excellence on the people side.

The women we interviewed were comfortable knowing that someone else in the organization understood the numbers, so they did not need to have those figures immediately at hand. "I know my sales operations person has all that data," said Corrine Perritano, executive vice president—direct to consumer business, at Jenny Craig, Inc. "If I need to make a decision, I look at the data real time. I am able to drive results in the moment."

This variance in viewpoints may be a key factor in explaining why CEOs historically have not believed that females in sales have the same grasp of important numerical concepts as do males in similar positions. Visualize the following hypothetical scenario: Company A conducts the obligatory second quarter earnings call. Representing the Company are the CEO, the chief financial officer and the lead investor relations person. Also participating on the call are institutional holders of Company A's stock. The investor relations executive warns everyone about the risk of forward looking statements. The CEO reports on revenue, earnings and progress on stated key performance indicators, and then turns the call over to the chief financial officer for details. The numbers now center on receivables outstanding, inventory turns and non-cash stock option expense. The investor relations person then opens the call to questions. First up is the lead analyst from a prominent investment banking firm: "If I back into the revenue figures and compare them to competitors one, two, and three, it looks like you lost about 2.31 percent market share this quarter. This is up from our estimated market share loss figure from first quarter of 1.69 percent. Can you forecast for me if this is a trend, and could we expect next quarter's market share loss to be at the same pace, resulting in a share loss of 2.93 percent?"

After a long, silent pause, the CEO interrupts the panicking finance chief and says, "I do not know. I do not focus on the details around market share figures, but I have people in the Company who do. If you give me some time I will get you the figures you require." Before the teleconference concludes, the investment banking firm's analyst has issued a new earnings estimate for third quarter, reflecting much lower earnings per share. He cites Company A's poor understanding of future market share losses and its inability to translate them into revised profit forecasts. The new estimate, propelled by the viral nature of the Internet, causes all 27 analysts covering the stock to rapidly revise down future profit estimates. Moments later, the Company loses 10 percent of its market value.

Is this scenario extreme? Maybe. However, such is the world of the CEO. He is the boss of the chief sales executive. Therefore, if a female who wants to be a chief sales executive cannot answer the numbers questions when asked, on the spot, her chances of getting or retaining the top job are slim. For some reason, men seem to understand this unwritten requirement, but many women do not. To be a serious contender for the top spot, a woman must enter the ring with all the numbers at her fingertips.

Interactions vs. Relationships

Judy Fick, of Unisys, realized while working toward her Ph.D. in organizational design that CEOs are usually either great at numbers or people, but not both. The same seems to apply to chief sales executives. To be an effective sales leader, Fick says, "You have to enjoy engaging with people all the time. They can't be a distraction."

Women often have the skills to build relationships. Their softer, empathetic touch makes them "likable," admittedly a subjective term. But if you are likable to a client, your peers or your boss, you can more easily build what Fick calls "customer intimacy." Today's women can speak on a variety of topics, including sports, and are often more accomplished in the relationship-building process. Of course, Fick notes, you need the track record to support your customer relationship skills. The boss and your team must know you can deliver—not just build great relationships.

While men tend to focus on specific fact-finding or sharing interactions with associates to maintain operating excellence— conversations about numbers of transactions, conversions and quarterly results—women interact with associates for the sake of building and nurturing long-term relationships which become the platform or infrastructure for achieving excellence. Numbers are integral to the conversation, but not the foundation.

"Men interact on the business issues, while women look at the whole issue personally and professionally," reflects Karen Bressner, senior vice president for advertising sales at TiVo Inc. "To make a big decision, women seek broader and less exclusive counsel than do men. A woman might talk to ten other women, and men to only three other men," she continues. "Women count on feelings of their peers more than do men. They deal with the emotional aspects, not just the business parts. It is not that one way is better, just different."

Tangibles vs. Intangibles

Historically, men have been able to sell tangible, hardware-based products and services, where few women have seemed to thrive. Traditional lines of manufacturing, construction and technology continue to hire mostly numbers-oriented male salespeople.

For example, gender imbalance in the sales work force caught the attention of the *Wall Street Journal*, which profiled in a recent article the apparent discriminatory sales hiring practices of EMC, a global technology leader. In 2007, EMC fielded a sales force of 86.5 percent males and 13.5 percent females (up from 8.3 percent in 2004).[51] Change is in the wind, however.

The article also quotes Kelly Harman, managing director of Zephyr Strategy. "Tech sales used to be a very testosterone-laden environment, like playing for a football team," Harman recalls. "You had a bunch of white guys running around selling technology. They would say, 'We won't change just to make you (women) comfortable.'"[52]

---

[51] Bulkeley, *Wall Street Journal*, A1.

[52] Bulkeley, A1.

Through the lens of her role as sales group chairwoman of Women in Technology (WIT), a national professional organization, Harman sees a growing number of technology companies working to create a more balanced sales force. One reason for this trend may be that women seem to rank as the preferred gender for selling intangibles that more directly involve people. Examples include training and development services, human resources programs, information technology solutions, marketing services or consulting solutions.[53]

"Men tell customers all about their product's features—facts and numbers, feeds and speeds, the numerical impact it will have on the prospect's company," observes Mary Delaney of CareerBuilder. com. "But women tell stories about the effect their product has had on a buyer and that company. They deal in intangibles." Remember

Network vs. Networking

NANCY SELLS
Senior Vice President Sales Strategy and Implementation
PR Newswire Association, LLC

Sells believes one of her keys to success is a strategic approach to selling. Self-taught, she realized early that sales is not about taking orders. Long before networking was a common term, she discovered that the people she knew could help her drive more revenue. Sells did not always understand why she met the people she met, but she knew that building a long-term relationship was much more important than approaching every encounter with the attitude of "what can you do for me today." She intentionally and purposefully stays in touch with many long-time acquaintances. "These are people who still today can help sway deals for me. It is about understanding the value of your network, not the value of networking."

---

[53] Rob Halvorsen, Contributing Writer, "Top Sales Careers for Women," *Sales Careers Online*, http://www. salescareersonline.com/articles/article_08022006.html.

the author's experience as a very young female selling manufacturing systems to gruff plant managers? It was the stories of other plant managers' successes that earned her credibility in this male-dominated world despite her youth and gender, not the "feeds and speeds" of the hardware or the eloquence of the programming code.

Delaney reflects this philosophy in leading her team meetings. "It's a waste of time for the sales team to go over forecasts or last month's numbers. The more you talk about numbers, the less those numbers will happen," she says. "The time to talk numbers is one-on-one and not in a group. Group meetings should be about people—time to develop skills, to strategize about accounts or people, to make career development plans for the team."

Delaney adds, "I praise my top performers. Yes, sales performance is based ultimately on numbers, but my top performers are not always the top numbers people. The numbers happen because we take care of people. Numbers are short-term. People are our growth infrastructure. We can endure only if we develop and grow our people."

CHAPTER 9

Purpose and Passion

The women we interviewed started their climb up the sales ladder primarily in the late 1970s and early 1980s, for the executive level requires years of formative experience. Most of these women have changed companies only once or twice during their entire sales career. Of those interviewed, 86 percent reached the chief sales executive position in the same company in which they began their career.

In general, women tend to view their lives from a more holistic perspective than do men. In Chapter 4, we looked at how female leaders embrace and engage their many roles as wife, mother, breadwinner, executive, mentor and more, and make calculated choices over the life of a career. Women have an innate ability to see what lies up the road, as well as on both sides, behind, below and above them, all at the same time. The childhood mantra that "mothers have eyes in the back of their heads" speaks to the recognized existence of this uniquely female attribute. But, do not assume that this powerful radar works only at home. At the office, the "mom" arrives with antennae discreetly raised, a hypervigilant bundle of 360-degree sensory omniscience, marching along her career path with purpose and passion, all the while alert to nuances in interpersonal relationships with colleagues and clients.

Motivation Unleashed

"I can motivate and inspire a sales team, and I also have the ability to lead and manage change. Those are my strengths as a chief sales executive," states Deb Gallagher of Pinnacle Selling. "I'm good at business planning. I focus and execute well. I have courage, by which I mean commitment and follow-through. I collaborate well with customers. And, I manage the leading indicators of success."

Management came naturally to her, but she had to work at developing leadership abilities, Gallagher confides. She found that to be a truly effective chief sales leader, one must lead, motivate and inspire the sales organization. To do that, she says, requires several key attributes.

"First, you must have a passion for sales. What I love about sales is that I really get out and solve problems that affect business outcomes and the customer. To me that is everything. Second, I'm objective-driven. I stay very focused on sales objectives, the metrics and the business planning that go behind them. Third is being process-driven. That means having methodology, sales processes and best practices, then having processes around account acquisition, customer acquisition, deal planning, partner planning and all the other aspects. And, through it all, be collaborative. Develop the ability to establish trust and credibility with customer executives."

Hanging Tough

One reason for their strong, global awareness may be that women function as the renewing, reproductive, regenerating force of our society. The imperative to produce, nurture, protect and develop the next generation becomes the over-arching context for all other concerns, including careers. Indeed, the commentaries we heard suggest that women tend to view professions in a wider scope and longer term than do men. Females typically respond with greater flexibility and adaptability to career changes within a company, so long as those opportunities keep them moving toward their long-term life goals.

This explains, in part, why women change jobs less frequently than do men. As previously mentioned, the average male chief sales executive changes jobs every 19 months, with higher income, additional perks and a stronger career title each time. By contrast, females tend to stay in a single organization and grow their way to the chief sales executive position, reaching the top spot after 25 to 30 years with that same company, on average.[54] These figures suggest that, compared to men, women take longer to reach the top sales job and are passed over or opt-out of contention more frequently. Much of that can be attributed to the lifestyle decisions described in previous chapters. But, a little cheerleading along the way can help, says Cathy Perry, professional certified coach and founder of InwardBound Coaching.

"Take the woman toughing it out and doing a good job in entry-level sales," Perry says. "What can happen to her attitude when somebody she respects pulls her aside and says, 'You definitely could be a VP of Sales around here. Let me work with you in the weeks and months ahead and bring other people in to also work with you, to show you how that looks and what it is going to take.' What affirmation that is! Men would like that, too, but I believe that women with the ability need more affirmation that they can do the job. Men may interpret the female need for affirmation as lack of confidence or lack of commitment,

---

[54] Hrehocik, "Best Sales Force," citing Alexander survey.

but it is neither. It's just noticing and acknowledging the ability that she has."

Slow and Steady

Most women take a conservative stance when considering next steps inside or outside a company. They calculate the risk of staying in one company that will support their overall life plan versus the more daunting risk of moving on and up. Staying with the current company may present fewer promotional opportunities for a woman, with slower advancement. However, taking a higher level position elsewhere means having to prove herself again and learning a new culture, thus demanding more of that ever-valuable personal or family time.

It is logical to assume that a woman may choose to stay with a good employer who knows her skills and successes, and is willing to invest in her for the

Extraordinary Women

JUDY FICK
Vice President and General Manager, Worldwide Sales
Unisys

Fick's father, an automotive industry executive, and his colleagues served as her earliest role models for a sales career. "When he and his friends from work got together, I would observe who looked the happiest," she says. "Then I would ask them what they did. The happiest were in sales and traveled all over the world. I knew then I wanted that lifestyle and that sales was the way to have it!"

To this day, she uses that same power of observation and discernment to read clients and prospects, as well as strong sales candidates.

Fick calls herself "a student of powerful women." Always an avid reader, she drew inspiration from books about life experiences of women who stood out in the time, place and role they played. "I read many biographies of women like Amelia Earhart and Margaret Thatcher, who were truly pioneers in their respective fields. They were extraordinary women in extraordinary roles that were not traditional for women of their era. These women made a mark in history."

She met one of these female pioneers one summer, serving as a page to then Prime Minister Margaret Thatcher. "Mrs. Thatcher was an amazing woman," Fick says. "I learned again that gender makes no difference in my ability to succeed."

long term. She may reluctantly forego an immediate pay increase by not jumping to another company, but she knows just staying gives her an advantage; both she and the company already know and trust each other.

Corrine Perritano, of Jenny Craig, praises her employer for taking Perritano's teaching skills and adapting them from training to sales skills. Over the years, each new job gave her on-the-job training and internal credibility, opportunities she doubts would have existed in a different company. Now at the top of her game, she has the credentials that make her a sought-after commodity. However, she emphasizes that it would take a lot for her to leave the company that has trained and nurtured her over the last 15 years.

Calculated Risk vs. Risk Avoidance

Women tend to lay out the big picture and then plan the details of the next step, a strategy they also employ in career planning. An example comes from one of our interviewees whose résumé includes several chief sales executive positions and who is currently competing for the president's job at a $100M company. Early in her career, she defined her ideal role and calculated that she would need new developmental experiences every five years in order to become a president or CEO by age 45. Being a realist, she allotted one set of those five-year steps as time to have her children. And, in order to gain the skills she had determined were necessary to attain her goals, she found she needed to change companies every couple of years. While changing jobs frequently seems to have worked well for her, the norm for women is less nomadic.

Men show far more interest in switching companies in order to move up. In the Information Technology industry in the 1970s, the typical tenure of a good programmer was less than a year. Why? Were there that many awful employers? Were programmers that irresponsible? No, the answer was the pocketbook power of job-hopping.

Good talent in the burgeoning IT world was scarce, so employers offered significant salary bumps to anyone who would jump ship and join their company. Back then, men held most of these jobs, and they seemed to have no remorse at leaving an employer in the lurch for the sake of a salary increase. One sales professional we talked with in casting our net for female leaders confessed that she jumped off the sales management ladder when she realized that her goal was not to become a sales executive, but instead to "make mountains of money" over the next ten years, then invest in a second life as an entrepreneur. Few endeavors present more risk than becoming an entrepreneur. That goal was a decade out, but she chose to carefully lay out a career development plan that would allow her to build the financial resources and the skills she would need to be successful in her chosen path. In comparison, the research shows men feel less inclined to think in these progressive terms beyond one year, much less ten years down the road.

In the current business climate, it appears that women in sales positions feel even less inclined to switch jobs despite the short-term increase in salary. Are women fearful of change? Creatures of habit? Risk avoiders? Calculated risk takers? Or are they just more loyal to the company? For Cathy Perry of InwardBound Coaching, it all boils down to knowing who you are.

"There is something about a woman owning her accomplishments easily and powerfully that sends the message, 'I so belong here,'" Perry says. "When she can communicate that, the power of leadership starts with her. Rather than wondering what her boss can do for her, she might ask what can she do for herself—what risks can she take—by tapping into her own power? That the CEO empowers her to take risks would be a great sign. Risk taking is such a critical part of leadership. If we have the leeway, the rope, the resources and the support to take risks, then we are set up to succeed."

CHAPTER 10

Leadership

Women and men both have what it takes to lead others. From earliest history to present day, leaders of both genders have exhibited a sense of purpose, strong instincts, insights and passion. Yet, very real differences in style between men and women drive their distinctive approaches to dealing with people.

Overall, our women interviewees *believe their holistic approach to leading a major sales organization is a positive factor and differentiates them from men.* They attribute this broad, inclusive view to natural instincts of caring for the family and home as ingrained in womankind since the cave man days. Nurturing and caring for hearth and home seem to come naturally to women, even, and maybe especially, to women in strong sales leadership roles.

Strategy at 30,000 Feet

One senior global sales executive started her career at the company as a systems engineer. Now, two decades later, running a major piece of the company's business, she still applies her engineering mind to sales. She turns potentially wasted airplane commuting hours into time for strategic deliberation about her business. "I have to step back to get beyond just improving the current processes," she says. "Maybe we need to be using different and new processes instead of improved versions of what we are already doing."

The executive describes three major components of her leadership style. First, the engineering mindset—she looks at the situation as a problem to be solved. Second, she looks at the organizational piece and breaks down the big picture into processes and components, using metrics she can track on a monthly basis. She then lists necessary activities and time projections over the multi-year life cycle of the project. Her third component—caring for and nurturing relationships with both her team and customers.

"I come to work thinking of these things, but it is hard for me to tell if my male counterparts are doing the same or not," she confides. The fact that male sales managers ask her how she has turned around failing business units and built new ones so quickly suggests that the men have not caught on to her methods. The good news is that they want to learn her secret.

Big Picture and the Details

Planning strategically, along with managing the details, surfaced as recurring strengths among women sales executives in our study. While many men also pay attention to detail, most of our interviewees believe this is more of a female strength and one that sets them apart from their male peers.

Dorane Wintermeyer, vice president, sales, Regence Blue Cross Blue Shield of Oregon, was the only woman in the field early in her career. She cites the value of both strategy and attention to detail as the keys to her success. "The guys would laugh at me, because at client presentations, I would have done a lot of research before going on the call," she relates. "I would have a printed agenda, with everything set up at clean right angles, the business cards lined up in the right order––everything had an order and there was a reason behind that order. Women pay attention to the details, and the details make a difference."

Wintermeyer is convinced that her preparation and attention to detail eventually earned her the top sales executive position. She competed for the job against a man, as she always had, but she was the one who had done the homework, and that made the difference. Her current boss, a male, appreciates the fact that the women on his team can pay attention to the details, as well as think strategically. Wintermeyer believes that you have to have the big picture in mind when you are managing a deal, but also keep all the pieces in mind. "Never assume the 'i's are dotted and the 't's are crossed until you know they are."

Today, when she stands before a group, she believes one of her key differentiators is still that attention to detail. Wintermeyer also makes sure all tactical items get completed after the meeting. "Follow-up is a commitment you make to do something for someone else in that meeting," she says. "Women seem to listen better. If I watch a room full of people in a meeting, most people aren't listening. They are waiting for someone else to stop talking so that they can talk. I try to take in everything, the non-verbal clues and behaviors, as well as the words. Listening and accurate, timely follow-up make the difference."

Lisa Cutts, of Misys Healthcare, believes one of the traits her male boss most appreciates is her ability to think strategically and act tactically. Her strengths in listening instead of talking allow her to take in non-verbal cues that a more aggressive "seller" might miss because he or she was talking. Lisa analyzes herself after every event. "I want to know what worked and what didn't work. Paying attention to the details before, during and after a call outlines my homework and allows me to be fully prepared for the next call. I don't know a lot of men, in or out of sales, who go to the same depth of detail."

Teamwork vs. Stardom

As previously noted, women seem to focus more of their energies on building a team for the long haul than on the immediate numbers and quotas. Dorane Wintermeyer exemplifies this attitude and says, "Building the team for the long term is much more important than a few quick wins. I don't want a basketball team with one star. I want a team that works together." As a result, women place greater emphasis on charting a career within a given company, or externally with a potential future employer, based on a life view instead of a more limited career view. Because that broad view is important to them, they tend to emphasize the same with their teams.

Sales leaders need to assemble and develop their teams for the long haul. The team infrastructure may take years to cultivate, and focusing on quarter-to-quarter numbers can blind the leader to crevasses looming ahead. Defining top performers as those who show a balance of long- and short-term outlooks, both as individuals and as leaders and developers of their own teams, ensures continuous skills development, in addition to numeric goals attainment.

"Women are more likely to take the time to develop relationships," Wintermeyer adds. "They are willing to give others the credit, and to invest in people, especially at the hiring stage. But they are not afraid to cut bait with non-performers when the time comes. On the other hand, few men rarely take an interest in another person outside of just the cursory."

How vs. What

Our research found that women start with the "how" to get something done, whereas men care more about "what" to do. Responding to questions about talent in general, women more often talk about how they recruit people, rather than jumping to turnover statistics. Women first examine a person's style, values and attitude—all more intuitive, nurturing type traits—and then work up to the numbers.

"I recruit for optimism, a generally positive outlook on life," declares Wintermeyer. "I can teach people product, process and skills, but I can't take someone who is negative on life and turn that person into a successful salesperson or sales leader." When Wintermeyer became chief sales executive, turnover at the company was at a high of 58 percent, some of which was involuntary. Since she took the job, no key executives have left, and turnover among the sales force plummeted to less than 15 percent. Her secret? She looks at the person, as well as the numbers.

To develop talent, Wintermeyer measures both the "what" and the "how." She assesses the success of her team based equally upon measurement of achievement against the goals and subjective evaluation on how well they worked as a team. "To be successful in sales and sales leadership, you need to balance both," she says.

Playing with the Boys

Key to successful leadership is the drive to engage with all segments of the customer base and work force on their own turf.

For female leaders in particular, that means playing ball with the boys.

So, welcome to the "good ol' boys' club." Or, for women, "Enter at your own risk." Whether it is a golf course, country club or gentlemen's club, almost every woman we interviewed identified at least one traditional all-male venue that comes as a perk with the chief sales executive job. For a woman, these environments present choices about lifestyle––whether to participate, how often and what role to take.

Although many of our interviewees said they do not feel a need to attend traditional male bonding events, the reality is that good ol' boys' clubs do present unique opportunities for women to strengthen crucial social and business connections with their male colleagues and clients. Indeed, when asked to name the number one impediment holding them

Working for a Man or a Woman

HEIDI GAUTIER
Vice President, U.S. Commercial Operations, Endocrine Business Unit
Genzyme Corporation

Gautier works on an all-male executive team in a pharmaceutical company. Her industry is known for hiring women salespeople, but the female ranks get thin at the top. "I have heard many times that a female boss is either the absolute worst boss a woman could have or the very best. It just depends on that woman's level of security and self-confidence. Any woman who is going to walk into a room full of men had better be confident that she can handle any situation that comes along."

Though Gautier would like to believe that the glass ceiling is a thing of the past, she knows there is still room at the top for good women and it remains tough to get there. She works hard and hopes she is setting a role model for younger women, including her daughters. "I tell my daughters all the time, 'I hope this is the right example I am setting for you guys.'" Even her reference to her girls as 'guys' seems to show she sees men and women as equally eligible and competent for the job, whatever it may be.

back from executive roles, the frequent hesitant reply came as, "I don't play golf well enough," or "I don't entertain the men the same way my male counterparts would."

Said in jest by some women but seriously by others, the traditional belief that deals are done on the golf course appears to be alive and well among the current generation of women sales leaders. Playing golf with the "guys," for example, allows the "gals" to join in impromptu strategy sessions or to bond in other ways. Having few other women to hobnob with along the way, it is no surprise that more female leaders and aspiring executives are taking up golf or dining out more often with male clients and peers. These females grew up usually the lone woman in a "man's world," whether in front line sales or sales management.

"In mentoring men, I can point them in the right direction and they run with it," observes Rebecca Bernson, senior vice president, national accounts sales for Automatic Data Processing, Inc. (ADP). "Men already know the guys that are on the radar for promotion or assignment into other jobs. But women are not even on the radar, so as a senior woman, I have to be their cheerleader. I have to teach them PR. They have to talk up each other, because they just are not top-of-mind for advancement."

Men may not even realize how closed the door is to their women peers. Nevertheless, women are painfully aware of important conversations they never even hear about that have occurred on the golf course, at the club, or over a good cigar after dinner, because they were not aware of the event, nor were they invited.

While the point can be made that each gender naturally congregates together, as is demonstrated repeatedly in strictly social groups, the counterpoint says that social-business settings should reflect the diverse makeup of the organization, which does include women. After all, to those of either gender on their way to the top, the line between social and business becomes blurred. With so much time and energy expended on developing relationships, the merging of the two facets cannot be avoided. Therefore, the more time spent with the broad spectrum of both company and client individuals, the more each sales professional will learn and enhance his or her career.

Women who choose to mingle with their male peers quickly learn the first rule of the game: if you play with the boys, do it well, the same way you do your job well. Some women already possess a passion and skill for golf, so the choice to join in the competition with men may be easy. A novice, however, may want to take a cram course to hone her skills before exposing her inexperience on the links (as the author once tried with the utmost short-term success, moving her at least temporarily from the role of drink hostess to peer). That, of course, means even more time away from hearth and home.

The second rule of the game is this: anyone—male or female—who enters the good ol' boys' club environment should not be surprised by the occasional off-color joke, innuendo or behavior. Indeed, women often find the conversation at these events to be less than refreshing. One study participant said that after one particular such occasion, she felt as though she needed a shower, she felt so debased and dirty.

Says Stacey Reid of Chantal Corp., "You've heard the Las Vegas slogan, 'What happens in Vegas, stays in Vegas.' Well, that is how it works in the good ol' boys' clubs. No one talks about these indiscretions." In one extreme example, a female chief sales executive refused a request to give her male sales representatives hundred-dollar bills to pay for strippers and even prostitutes. She agrees that recent harassment legislation has considerably toned down this kind of antic, but it does happen. Most men likely would also find this sort of behavior offensive. Today, these activities may still take place but are more likely to be disguised as expense items related to entertainment for reps or customers at conferences and conventions.

Regardless of setting or intent, says Dorane Wintermeyer, "If someone is disrespectful to you personally, let that person know you don't appreciate it. Otherwise, sometimes you have to just accept that it is the way it is, not take offense, and keep on moving."

In spite of these kinds of challenges along the way, the fruits of engaging, inclusive leadership can be enormous. One woman executive describes how she took up smoking cigars early in her sales days more than 20 years ago, just to gain entrance into the inner sanctum of men's discussions. She is still known as "the woman who smokes cigars with the guys." Yet, the strategy of engaging with her male peers paid off. In just ten years, she advanced her career, achieved her leadership goals, grew her company and ultimately took it public.

In summary, women sales leaders seem to view their role as facilitator and enabler of their teams and the individuals on those teams as opposed to being the star individual for others to follow. They draw the attention away from themselves and the results and focus instead on the infrastructure and individuals that allow them to accomplish the end results. The long-term view and attention to the processes and details necessary to reach the objectives have paid off for the female chief sales executives we interviewed.

CHAPTER 11

Intentional Mentoring

Life is a journey of learning. From an early age, we learn skills, facts, figures, rules and behaviors. We receive instruction at home, school, church, clubs and summer camps. We absorb information from the Internet, friends, books, movies, television, radio, magazines and newspapers. In the business world, we continue to learn from on-the-job experience, training courses and policy manuals. We conduct research, pick up on cultural cues and try to figure out what works well and what does not.

This hodge-podge of accumulated knowledge, however, often gives us only unconnected information and data, without context or meaning. In the business world, what we learn helps us tread water, but not to swim.

And then, there is mentoring.

Those unfamiliar with the practice may perceive mentoring as just another trendy buzzword floating around, a process with the same benefit as a training course, the company newsletter or a crystal ball. Or perhaps they view mentoring as some kind of strange, obscure management ritual practiced in secret.

It is none of these.

Simply put, mentoring is a one-to-one relationship between a "mentor"—the individual with experience to share, and a "mentee"—the person with a desire to gain insights from the mentor. The mentor guides the mentee to new insights, enabling the mentee to discern what is and is not important in the context of their developing career. The mentor helps the mentee find direction. And then, to swim.

Mentoring differs from its cousin, role modeling, because of the addition of the personal interaction factor. A role model can be anyone that a person looks up to and emulates—parent, teacher, manager, movie star, statesperson or medical pioneer. Any of these may also be a mentor, but only if a personal, interactive and ongoing relationship exists with the mentee.

The World Needs Mentors

The need for effective mentors continues to grow in the business world, especially for those in the field of sales. A 1996 Catalyst study showed that women cited lack of access to mentors as a serious barrier to career advancement.[55] A 2006 survey by the Simmons School of Management showed that the use of mentors has significantly increased. Sixty percent of the women in the study who had mentors reported that their mentors were women. Seventy-one percent of the women in the study reported that they themselves served as mentors.[56] As senior salespeople and executives retire, many of the 5 million women currently in entry-level sales positions, along with incoming Millennial

[55] "Mentors of Women, by Women, for Women Growing in Importance, National Survey Indicates," *Business Wire,* February 3, 2003, cited Catalyst, 1996, study on women corporate leaders.

[56] "Mentors of Women, by Women, for Women Growing in Importance, National Survey Indicates," *Business Wire,* February 3, 2003, cited Simmons School of Management.

workers, will want to advance.[57] "Just about every successful woman I know has a good mentor or mentors," observes Deb Gallagher of Pinnacle Selling. "That is another advantage that men have over women; they have more mentors. I say behind every good woman is a good mentor. The same was true for me. As a result, I look forward to giving back to the community in organizations that are about teaching young people."

One surprise finding in our study is that women, and the men they work with, both seem to be blind to gender differences among themselves and the people they lead. Nearly every woman leader said she focuses on how to mentor the next generation of sales leaders—period—not only women sales leaders. Why? Because the up-and-coming Millennial generation is even more gender-blind than are these pioneering women executives. These youths seek to learn from wise elders, not caring whether the sages are male or female.

Many women we interviewed have never worked for another woman, and few have ever competed with a woman for any job. Therefore, it is no surprise that few women possess the full range of experience and background to mentor the next generation of sales leaders. However, they do carry an inherent desire to nurture and develop others. All of this said, *how will the current generation of middle-aged female sales leaders help develop their successors, male or female?*

Options do exist for women to mentor the next generation; they need only plug in and begin. To be an effective mentor for rising Millennials, a senior sales leader must first build a personal foundation for intentional, purposeful behavior in every aspect of life. The first layer of that foundation will be a consistent, day-to-day, goal-driven

---

[57] "101 Facts on Workingwomen," 2.

lifestyle in business and personal affairs. As we have noted, Millennials are not only interested in the business side of their mentors. They do not want to know how to build a career to the exclusion of a life outside work. They want to know that success can be defined in a broad array of life experiences and adventures. They will select as mentors those who demonstrate by their actions a real understanding and achievement of the new kind of success. Once this more holistic success foundation has been cemented, young saleswomen can confidently make mentoring choices that best suit their talents, aspirations and needs.

Voluntary Mentoring

Most executives ease into mentoring through one of many volunteer programs that exist both inside and outside corporations. A program may be purely voluntary for the mentor and mentee, or the mentee may pay for an outside organization to coordinate the mentoring. Both approaches aim to help women break through the middle levels of management by matching aspiring young sales leaders and managers with seasoned executives. Pairing methods are almost limitless, but many match a female chief sales executive with a sales leader in her organization or in a similar, but not competitive, industry.

Internal mentoring match-ups enable mentees to develop skills and characteristics needed to achieve success within that specific organization. This mentoring approach is on the rise inside large corporations such as GE, Microsoft and IBM.[58] In these programs, women at more senior levels pair up by function or discipline with

---

[58] "Corporate Mentoring Programs on the Upswing," Society for Industrial and Organizational Psychology (SIOP) news release, October 11, 2006. http://www.newswise.com/articles/view/524216/.

inexperienced employees, outside either one's reporting hierarchy. Sometimes, the match centers on a specific career stage or obstacle that the mentor has experienced, and that the mentee is facing. Many programs suggest that pairs set a specific goal for the mentee, for example, to achieve a new position, win an account, begin a new behavior or acquire a new skill before the formal mentoring relationship ends.

Most pairings last for a set period of time, usually a year, with two or three measurable objectives per year. Most pairs hold monthly, two-hour, face-to-face meetings, with occasional email or telephone contact in between. They agree on actions to be completed between meetings, such as the mentor's observing a mentee's behavior in a certain situation and discussing what could be done differently to achieve other results. Occasionally, a serendipitous bond occurs between the two women, above and beyond the normal short-term coaching rapport, and a career-long mentoring bond is forged. These latter types of relationships can prove very valuable to both parties, as both continue to learn from and motivate each other during various career stages.

Lack of time can become an issue because the mentors most in demand tend to be the busiest. Yet, these women view mentoring as a part of their job and generally make a real effort to ensure consistent contact with and availability to their mentee(s). Baby Boomer chief sales executives are eager to equip Millennials with the savvy and skills necessary to quickly step into the shoes of the retiring generation.

Succession Mentoring

Careful succession planning helps executives identify candidates most in need of mentoring, and who will provide the highest return on investment of their time, energy and resources. Indeed, mentoring and grooming one's successor at the very top of an organization can pay huge dividends, as the leaders of Xerox describe in a recent issue of *Fortune* magazine. The article highlights women who intentionally mentor other women to replace themselves or advance to another leadership role. Featured on the cover are mentor Ann Mulcahy and mentee Ursula Burns, respectively CEO and president of Xerox. Their mentoring relationship began when they arrived at the helm of the ailing company and realized they needed to help each other to turn the ship around. They stabilized the leaky vessel and began to grow a large business in an industry battered by a tumultuous sea of change.[59]

You Can Go Anywhere!

ANNE KAISER
Senior *Vice President, Customer Support and Sales*
Georgia Power
(Unit of Southern Company)

Kaiser's father, a veteran of many years at General Electric Corp., had some advice for his daughter, based on his own first-hand experience. Although trained in engineering, where he spent much of his career, he first learned to sell. She heard her father say, "Anne, if you get a job in sales, you can go anywhere."

She took his advice. Armed with a combined journalism and public relations degree, her first job out of college was selling paper to university book stores. Kaiser says she has been selling ever since, regardless of what her actual title has been!

What does it take to groom your successor, whether male or female? Mulcahy notes, "There is a lot of emotion involved, and it has nothing to do with being a woman. It's there for all of us, and the question is, do you deal with it or don't you?"[60]

---

[59] Betsy Morris, "The New Buddy Act," *Fortune*, October 15, 2007, 76.
[60] Morris, 81.

During their early days as a leadership duo, they divided sales and operations functions, and, more importantly, problem solving. Dealing with egos, they admit, was difficult but critical. At one turbulent point, Burns proposed the traditional organization chart with everyone reporting to the president and the president reporting to the CEO, to which Mulcahy replied, "What the heck will I do!?"[61] They resolved that issue by dividing the problems instead of the functions. Burns is the ultimate operations problem solver while Mulcahy is masterful with customers. As a team, each is able to play to her strengths and mentor the other in her weaker areas, yielding the maximum result for the company. Their solution did not come easily, but because of their mutual trust and respect, they were able to create a highly productive solution.

While neither woman's title became specifically sales, the role of revenue generation was at the center of the discussions preparing for the ultimate passing of the baton from Mulcahy to Burns. By whatever title, they were clear that a focus on sales had to come from the top.

Coaching

In days gone by, "coaching" was code for, "You messed up, and now we are going to try to straighten you out." No longer is coaching a punitive term. Today, companies offer coaching as a perk to executives at even the highest levels. With a succession plan in place, the chief sales executive can easily see who will benefit most from coaching and which skill sets a person needs to advance to the next position.

A formal coach, usually hired from outside the organization for the sake of objectivity, administers a review of what peers, subordinates

---

[61] Morris, 84.

and superiors believe to be the strengths and weaknesses of the person being coached, makes his or her own assessment of the employee's skills and provides feedback by outlining action steps that reinforce existing strengths and fortify areas of weakness. The coaching is accomplished in a way that teaches the client specific transferable skills necessary to succeed as an executive in sales or other fields of focus.

Informal coaching resembles mentoring, in which an experienced person inside the organization offers counsel to another person trying to overcome some obstacle. The coaching relationship is less structured than mentoring and may even be a one-time, spontaneous event. In the informal scenario, a mentor or coach with prior experience offers guidance to help the other person make the right decisions in order to move past an obstacle or to succeed at a goal. A recent study of informal coaching or mentoring by a more experienced salesperson of a less experienced salesperson found that job experience, job satisfaction, a measure of interpersonal competence, and role conflict are associated with willingness to mentor, while interpersonal competence and role conflict are associated with the actual ability to mentor.[62]

Mentoring Groups

As the need for mentoring increases, corporate-sponsored women's mentoring and networking groups are on the rise. External mentoring groups intentionally help women in middle management to break through the glass ceiling into the executive suite.

At one cross-functional mentoring organization, PathBuilders, corporations pay the private company an annual fee to match up their

---

[62] Ellen Bolman Pullins, Leslie M. Fine and Wendy L. Warren, "Identifying peer mentors in the sales force: An exploratory investigation of willingness and ability," *Journal of the Academy of Marketing Science*, 1996, vol. 24, no. 2, 127.

promising young female employees with older, wiser women in the same field. So, a rising female sales representative in pharmaceuticals may be paired with a female vice president of sales at a pharmaceutical company. The two would agree to spend two to four hours together each month for a year to share expectations, develop a career plan and work on specific weaknesses identified by assessment tools the group provides to younger women. Because the two women are not employer and employee, the relationship can be even more open and honest, protected by objectivity and anonymity. The organization also provides monthly educational programs, usually delivered by a successful woman on a topic of interest to all young women building a career. It is about women learning from women.

After a formal mentoring program ends, the mentor-mentee relationship may live on for years, in some cases moving to a peer-to-peer connection. In one case we learned of, the mentee eventually became the mentor's supervisor—a true instance of "the student becomes the teacher."

Good Mentoring Tips

Good mentors are good listeners, especially when interacting with the up-and-coming generation. "When we were young, we thought we had all the answers, too." says Beth Doherty of Emdigo, formerly a sales executive at Sony. "We were no more ready to hear an adult tell us they understood, and here is how you do it, than the current young generation is ready to hear that from us." As another woman put it, "My wisdom is not well received when it's handed down as an executive decision, so I do a lot of listening. I offer my thoughts as suggestions. Rather than pushing and shoving as the adult decision-maker, I let them learn on their own, just barely nudging them with quiet guidance. I give them permission to dream."[63]

Here are some tips for mentoring Millennials and others, from the experts we interviewed:

Do:

- Listen to their point of view.
- Appreciate their insights.
- Ask open-ended questions.
- Let their voice be heard.
- Discuss and brainstorm.
- Set up a scenario.
- Ask what an outcome might have been or should have been, and why.
- Have them blog or tap into their on-line community.
- Give them time and space to express criticisms.
- Let them wonder out loud how things could be done differently.
- Let them deliberate a question.
- Identify meaningful ways to measure performance.
- Give them choices.
- Present high expectations.
- Share personal experiences.

Avoid:

- Dumping information one-way.
- Declaring, "When I was your age, I did this or that."
- Stating, "Here's what I would do . . ."
- Preaching, "Here's what you should do . . ."
- Telling, not discussing and mutually discovering.

---

[63] Lisa Borden, "Next Gen Wants You," *Discipleship Journal*, NavPress®, May/June 2007:159, 47.

Section Three

MAKING IT HAPPEN

CHAPTER 12

Passing the Torch of Knowledge

Older workers are beginning to see life's road ahead as much shorter than the distance behind them. They quickly realize that someday "All This" will end. That insight, together with years of accumulated knowledge, experience, opinions and determinations, becomes elevated to the plane of wisdom.

For the eternally young-at-heart Baby Boomers in the work world, the term "senior position" now means something other than "executive level." As vessels of wisdom, they feel positioned to teach, lead, advise and serve as role models to the next generation. They are getting older, and they no longer need to keep that secret from everyone, including themselves.

But, while the mantle of "elder" may feel uncomfortable at first, Baby Boomers soon realize that their new status brings certain rewards and opportunities. After ruminating about the life lived thus far, time and again they focus on how to use their remaining years to benefit others. They find themselves called to pass along the knowledge gleaned from hard-won lessons to the next generation, in hopes of placing into those tender hands the means to carry on the work of making the world a better place.

This is no small task. In recent years, a new chief executive-level position called the chief learning officer has evolved. One chief learning officer currently recognized as a leading thinker, Dr. James J. L'Allier, suggests that companies facing the transition from Baby Boomer leaders to future Millennial leaders must proactively capture key competencies and critical work knowledge from employees before they retire. He calls for organizations to develop a strategic plan to position the entity for opportunity and growth as the wave of Baby Boomer retirees approaches.[64]

Companies face a hard irony, however. The aging work force possesses more stored knowledge and wisdom than any in world history. Yet, consistent with a law of nature, the members of the younger generation need to learn things for themselves, to reinvent the wheel just their way, to make their own mistakes in order to learn their own hard lessons.

In other words, the new generation does not want to use pre-packaged "solutions" based upon elders' past experience. Rather, elders must offer their insights and knowledge over time, to help youths develop into knowledgeable adults capable of making the right decisions for themselves and their organizations.

As never before, knowledge is power, and the information stored within the minds of the older generation grows less and less accessible with each passing day. Organizations must move quickly to capture and use this valuable resource, before the term "senior position" evokes a different image for elders—retirement homes and ocean cruises.

---

[64] Dr. James J. L'Allier, Ph.D. and Kenneth Kolosh, "Preparing for Baby Boomer Retirement," *CLO Magazine*, 2002.

Teach by Example

The affinity of women to nurture others and create relationships may explain why female executives easily engage Millennials in order to pass along their unique understanding of how women can advance in the workplace. One must remember that Millennials are a fast-paced generation. They grew up in a sound-byte world and very little keeps their attention for long. They expect life to be new and improved every day. It is important to help these young women see the new lessons in each new day, in each new situation.

Colleen Honan, of OneSource Information Services, mentors women and speaks frequently about leadership. To older women who want to pass along what they have learned in life, she offers this counsel, "Talk less and behave more." Simply stated, lead by example and teach by example.

While the older generation can lead and teach, she cautions, the plugged-in, savvy, younger generation must be willing to follow and learn from them in order to make the knowledge transfer happen. Therein lies a paradox; elders have much to teach, youngsters have much to learn, but the two often do not connect.

Indeed, the "we-know-it-all" malady affects both generations. Baby Boomers think they know it all because they have lived through so much. Millennials know they know it all and cannot be convinced otherwise, partially because their Baby Boomer parents have always encouraged them to think independently and not hesitate to voice their opinions. The old adage, "Children should be seen and not heard," was merely an archaic saying and definitely not a part of most Millennials' upbringing. However, another key to the Millennials' confident attitude comes from being the first generation in which the majority has recently completed not only high school, but additional years of formal schooling.

Only after digging into their first job does the bloom come off the rose for Millennials. Most of what they need to know in the real world was somehow omitted from the classroom (or perhaps they were absent that day, either mentally or physically, on some worthwhile adventure). With that in mind, Honan focuses on leading by example, and she offers sage advice to young salespeople. "Use your ears in proportion to your mouth. God gave us two ears and one mouth for a reason."

Aware that Millennials are used to digesting information in short, succinct, memorable formats, Honan gives them no more than three things to learn at a time. She brings the "listen and learn" axiom to life for younger workers. "I don't just tell them mechanics of making a cold sales call on the telephone," she says. "I pick up the phone and demonstrate what I am saying. I let them know I'm not asking them to do anything that I haven't done, or do, myself. I don't just tell them. I show them!"

Live and Learn

LISA CUTTS
Vice President, Sales
Misys Healthcare

Cutts grew up with two great role models in the family. Both of her parents were career people. Her sister is vice president of sales at a large retailer. Lisa is a part of an executive team that is one-half women. Still, she has never competed with another woman for a job. She believes that one of the biggest reasons there are not more women in sales leadership is their fear of not being able to do the job. To that end, Cutts is convinced that preparation, planning and listening before the call, listening and attention to non-verbal cues during the call, and critique and follow-up after the call are all critical. "Learning from what didn't go well is often the best way to improve. I still grade myself after each sales call or meeting." She encourages others to do the same. Learning is a life-long part of the job.

Teaching by example is a natural segue into the practice of mentoring discussed in Chapter 11. Both methods enable up-and-coming workers to learn from an older, more experienced leader. A female chief sales officer, for example, should consider the daily example she sets, as well as the formal mentoring process, as valuable methods of passing on knowledge and insights to those who may be considering their next move up in the organization.

Crumbs in the Classroom

With 21.6 percent of all U.S. college graduates having business majors[65] and more than 20 million people claiming sales as their profession,[66] the need for sales education is obvious.

But wait! There must be some mistake. Of the hundreds of educational institutions in the country, as of this writing only 20 offer a university-level major or minor degree in sales, and only five offer a graduate degree in sales.[67] *Ironically, the very function that brings in business revenue—sales—is one of the most difficult areas in which to obtain substantive training.* Sales is one of the least available degrees offered to aspiring business people. Educational institutions serve up a lavish banquet of degrees in almost every other business function—marketing, accounting, finance, entrepreneurism, organization development, human resources, management—but offer only crumbs in sales.

---

[65] "Number of U.S. Colleges and Universities and Degrees Awarded, 2005," *Infoplease©*, 2000–2007 Pearson Education, publishing as Infoplease, October 15, 2008, http://www.infoplease.com/ipa/A0908742.html.

[66] Vin Gupta, CEO, infoUSA, Omaha, NE, quoted in *Business Wire*, December 26, 2006.

[67] David Hoffmeister, The Sales Leadership Center, De Paul University, Chicago (www.salesleadershipcenter.com), interview, September 2007.

This dearth of basic sales training in academia means that individuals who want to learn sales or sales leadership skills have only three options—training provided by their company, courses at outside training companies or the tried and true "baptism by fire," also known as "sink or swim."

Fortunately, leading-edge educators and the business world are beginning to wake up to the value of formal sales leadership education. Several companies heavily fund and staff one of the earliest and most developed university sales programs, led by David Hoffmeister at De Paul University near Chicago.[68] The program leaders believe so strongly in the need for sales and sales management education that they offer assistance to any university desiring to develop a similar program. Business partners strongly support the program, seizing this opportunity to train future sales employees and to scout for emerging sales talent.

Another method that corporations might use to encourage sales education is to partner with a local high school system. For example, an early joint effort by American Express and Brooklyn's John Dewey High School created the Academy of Finance, inspired by Sandy Weill's 1982 vision for taking kids off the streets and onto Wall Street.[69] Although the Academy produced few recruits for American Express, more than 90 percent of the students graduated from high school, substantially more than in similar urban districts. Of those, 80 percent obtained two-year or four-year college degrees. Ten years later, 85 percent of them remained in white collar jobs, many of those sales-related.

---

[68] Hoffmeister interview.

[69] Elizabeth Svoboda, "Microsoft Class Action," *Fast Company*, September 2007, 86-95.

Today, Microsoft runs a similar successful program with the city schools of Philadelphia. Other companies, such as IBM, ExxonMobil, Chevron, Boeing, Dell, Google and Intel, also participate in various public/private school initiatives.

As the new model of public/private partnerships evolves, the high school classroom will become a place for women chief sales officers to share their experiences. And, as more colleges develop undergraduate and graduate programs to focus on and encourage sales as a profession, new opportunities will open up to teach and to recruit from a larger pool of sales-savvy young women.

Career Planning

Helping young women sales professionals develop career plans is an effective means for female sales leaders to pass on their experience. Women, who as we have seen take a more holistic view of their lives and careers than do men, can prompt discussions with younger workers about their interests, lifestyle preferences, and whether they would rather stay with one organization long term or seek faster promotions by hopping from company to company.

Millennials, already predisposed to job-hopping, closely resemble Baby Boomer men who built their careers by moving to a new job every 19 months to two years.[70] That kind of job-hopping may likewise help this generation of women get to the top faster than by staying in one place longer. Yet, the willingness to move frequently often depends on the lifestyle to which one aspires. And as we have seen, Millennials are predisposed to intertwine work and play in short segments and

---

[70] *Sales Benchmark Index*, survey.

see jobs as secondary to the fun and adventure those jobs enable them to experience.

How does a hiring manager find, encourage and retain those Millennial workers who are willing to work with the same ethic Baby Boomers expect? Working with those young people to create a career plan that may potentially even combine short tenures at a variety of companies may be a positive approach.

Colleen Honan of OneSource, who conducts the final telephone interviews with all sales candidates, admits that she views job-hopping as a sign of instability. "It is just way too expensive to hire a hopper," she states. "We give our people a lot of training. We can't make that investment unless we know the ROI [return on investment] is forthcoming."

Sometimes, to obtain objective views about career planning, the young worker may need to reach out for expert assistance, according to an article in *Employee Evolution*. "Seek professional help. No, not a psychologist, but a career coach or mentor, someone who has the experience and know-how to help you identify and pursue your unique vision of career success. You need to assess your strengths and get some guidance from an unbiased advisor. Your family or friends should not be your sole advice sources—they think everything you do is great and cannot be objective about what you should do to move forward. Another reason to turn to the experts is that many parents today (sorry Boomer Moms and Dads) provide their offspring with well-intentioned but sorely outdated career advice. And, some parents unfairly pressure their children to meet their own expectations of professional success. Instead, seek out a professional who can help you leverage your strengths and create a two-year plan that will let you feel focused and fulfilled."[71] Even the experts realize the wisdom of a shorter career plan—a two-year career planning horizon for the younger set instead of the five- or ten-year view of the Baby Boomer generation.

Strong organizations and strong leaders will continue to find ways to communicate their hard-won heritage with the next generation of leaders. Throughout the process, young people need to actively participate in their own development by working with an internal, senior level sales mentor to acquire the wisdom they need in order to reach their full potential.

---

[71] "Helicopter Managing Fails With Some Gen-Y & Corporate America's Pushing Back," *Work*, J.T., August 9, 2007, http://www.employeeevolution.com/archives/2007/08/09/helicopter-managing-fails-with-some-gen-y-corporate-americas-pushing-back/.

CHAPTER 13

Hiring and Promotion

It is decision time.

The hiring manager wades through résumés, compares their fit to the job description, interviews candidates, and consults with all the interested parties. Yet, the hiring decision carries consequences far beyond matching a name to a job slot. Every newly hired or promoted employee forever leaves a mark on the overall bench strength, competitive advantage and future success of the organization. That new employee may someday become the CEO, ruin the company through a wrong choice, or both.

The context for deciding who to hire or promote often goes back decades and reflects the economic imperatives of the time. In post-World War II America, waves of returning servicemen needed jobs, and companies needed manpower. Men queued up for the heavy lifting in factories and elsewhere to rejuvenate the economy. Women left those factory jobs they had entered out of war-time necessity and returned home to take care of the homes, nurture the next generation and repair the social fabric of family and community. In this way, the country lifted itself up by the bootstraps over the next half century to become the world's predominant economic powerhouse. The outcome was a strengthened economy that set the bar for the world's highest standard of living.

Today, the picture looks different, as U.S. companies grapple with new and complex forces that batter past assumptions from every direction—recessionary indications, mortgage crises, off-shoring, e-commerce, credit problems, trade imbalances, factory closings, shifting demographics, global competition, Baby Boomers retiring, Millennials rising, labor shortages, educational system strains and more.

These new realities cause hiring decision-makers to question the remnants of 1950s-era assumptions about the role of women and men in business. Today, as in the past, new economic forces dictate new approaches. Not just the male segment of society, but all hands are needed on deck. Company leaders are realizing they can no longer simply accept the dearth of female leadership if their organizations are to survive and prosper in the future.

Competitive Advantage

The body of work compiled over the last two decades about CEO effectiveness suggests the need for a new attitude in selecting business leaders. Jim Collins writes in *Good to Great* that "Level 5" leaders transform good companies into great companies. One way they do so is by hiring people unlike themselves.[72] These Level 5 leaders value diversity of opinion and understand that opposing views come across

---

[72] Jim Collins, *Good to Great*, HarperCollins Publishers Inc., New York, 2001, Chapter 2, 17-40, 2001.

more clearly when delivered by different kinds of people. The scarcity of female sales executives, and their unique perspective, presents a competitive advantage difficult to clone, given the supply and demand dynamics in the labor market. It takes a bold, fearless CEO to take the initiative and build up that competitive advantage.

CEOs value the diverse points of view of their management team members. Yet, when selecting the sales leader, decision-makers seem blinded by tradition and tend to hire men almost exclusively. How long will this old way of thinking hold the forces of progress at bay? What keeps this house of cards from crashing down?

One explanation may be that the scarcity of female contenders limits the chances of a woman being tapped. When male managers cast about for input on the next promotion or executive assignment, women are simply "out of sight, out of mind." Rarely can a woman's name be found on any executive search firm's short-list of candidates to fill a chief sales executive position. If executive search firms do not present women as applicants, then naturally the hiring executives will assume that there are no viable female candidates and will not consider women for those roles.

"I view people in my business as one of three things—outstanding individual contributors, outstanding sales managers or outstanding leaders," says Deb Gallagher of Pinnacle Selling. "In people I interview, I look for attributes of one of those three. As we know, too often we promote very strong individual sales contributors to management or a leadership role when they do not have the skills, the aptitude, the willingness or whatever to succeed. Looking for the right attribute is the key to making the best hiring decision."

Judy Fick, of Unisys, strives to maintain a gender-blind perspective when hiring. Explains Fick, "I never view the hiring process as a male-female competition, but more about finding the best person for the job. That's how I make my hiring and evaluation decisions, not based on gender. I'm so grateful my parents brought me up this way. Maybe the fact that I don't differentiate between the genders is my differentiator!" Oh, that more people could be that blind to the gender card!

The gender-blind view is supported by Heidi Gautier, vice president of U.S. commercial operations for the endocrine business unit of Genzyme Corporation, who says the male-female issue does not come into play in her search for talent. "I've had regional directors come and go, and I've replaced females with men and vice versa. My directors and sales team are split nearly 50-50, males to females," she says. "Our main focus is giving care to the patient, and we need to be very careful not to focus on the wrong things, but to concentrate on hiring the best talent. A female open to hiring great talent can be a great boss. On the other hand, a woman worried about losing her power base may be afraid to promote other women with talent. They surround themselves with men and can be very tough to work for. It all depends on her level of security and self-confidence."

Assumptions

When hiring workers, outmoded traditions and beliefs can have significant negative business impacts. A case in point is the recent job discrimination class action suit known as Dukes vs. Wal-Mart. In this case, the retailer was accused of discouraging promotion of women store employees to managerial positions and of paying them less than men across all job positions.[73]

---

[73] Roger Parloff, "The War Over Unconscious Bias," *Fortune*, vol. 156, no. 8, October 15, 2007, 92.

William Bielby, professor at the University of Illinois in Chicago, an expert for the plaintiffs in the case and a long-time student of gender segregation in the workplace, says that employers may unwittingly make bad decisions based upon what they assume to be a woman's preferred lifestyle.[74] Bielby suggests that managers unwittingly engage in "spontaneous" and "automatic" stereotyping and "in-group favoritism" that often results in the most desirable jobs being filled by people who look like the incumbents. The problem is not a company's policies; it is their managers' unwitting preferences. There are two likely scenarios for a situation such as the one in which Wal-Mart found itself, according to Bielby in a recent *Fortune* magazine interview.

The innocent possibility was that women sought out different jobs because of the responsibilities of raising children. They wanted lighter regular hours, no night shifts or weekends, and no geographic relocations. The perhaps unconsciously decided yet still illegal possibility was that managers were, at least to some degree, *assuming* that these would be women's preferences, inadvertently blocking those who *did* want more responsibility from ever getting it. As Bielby and like-minded others point out, studies show that "the strongest predictor of whether an opening is filled by a man or woman is whether the previous incumbent was a man or woman."[75]

Thus, a woman's preferences for lifestyle may be assumed to be those of previous generations simply because there has been nothing in the work force to negate that belief or cause a shift in thinking. As a result, no new opportunities to demonstrate a different set of lifestyle

---

[74] Parloff, 92.

[75] Parloff, 96.

values have occurred. It may be years before the courts can sort out the legal implications of hiring decisions based on perceived lifestyle preferences versus actual preferences. The lines may never be clear.

Difficult Career Choices

Traditionally, the perception has been that both men and women make career choices that reflect their gender. Men tend to think career first, without realizing that women see that as putting family second. "Simply being a woman makes hiring me a risk. With that as a starting point, it makes every other decision to advance a woman that much more difficult," says Beth Doherty of Emdigo.

"I know they are thinking early on that if they hire a woman rep, their investment will be wasted. So why bother. She will just take time off, or worse yet, quit to raise a family," adds Stacey Reid, of Chantal Corp. But it is a fact of life that if men are to have the children they want, it will require some number of women to be brave enough to make choices that could potentially sacrifice, or slow down, their career for the sake of family.

The up-and-coming generation may be more adept at solving the career/family dilemma than their predecessors. Millennials have aspirations that differ from those of their power- and success-driven Baby Boomer elders. Unlike individuals of their parents' generation, the identity of Millennials is not wrapped up solely in a job, but rather in how well-rounded they perceive themselves to be. What motivates them to work is not necessarily the status and power that might come with traditionally defined success.

Not that they are opposed to advancement, but they are more likely to work in order to fund what they do for fun. Life is an adventure. And not just any adventure. Many enjoy high adventure.

Be the Candidate; Get the Job

KAREN BRESSNER
*Senior Vice President,
Advertising Sales*
TiVo, Inc. (formerly MTV,
Home Entertainment)

Bressner has seen many women succeed with excellence in the jobs they pursued. Her mother set an early example as a teacher, sharing in the support of the family. "Watching my parents struggle financially drove me to be independent," she relates. "I knew I wanted the satisfaction of making it on my own."

She believes you get to the interview because of your ability and reputation, but often you are hired because of the people with whom you have worked over the past five, 10 and even 20 years. Since there are still more men in the upper echelons, she says "the odds are skewed against women" in high places. Bressner also notes that by its results-oriented nature, sales is an ideal place for strong, performance-driven women to climb the corporate ladder. In sales, results are easy to track and visible to all on any rung of the ladder.

Work may just be a way to pay for the next adventure, and much less about a career or long-term goal. As a result, these youths think little of working for a while, then leaving with little or no notice when the next adventure comes along or the first bump in the road arises.

The good news for chief sales executives is that sales is seen as a "cool" career to pursue. Colleen Honan, of OneSource, says that these new entries into the job market are attracted to sales because, "They can make a lot of money. It is highly competitive, but the money is good. However, for many of them, they want to make the money to be able to play, not to build for the long term or to provide for a family."

Promotion Hurdles

To qualify for the next rung on the ladder, companies often dictate how aspiring corporate leaders should spend their "own time" outside the normal 50-60 hour work week. Such lifestyle demands were the subject of the recent *Wall Street Journal* article about EMC Corp. mentioned in Chapter 8. A spokesperson reported that EMC heavily recruits former college athletes (a typically male-dominated selection pool) and "encourages their salesmen to call their best customers daily, give them small gifts and send them expensive bottles of wine when they dine out with their wives. Sales reps are expected to spend evenings dining with clients and weekends golfing with them."[76]

Unfortunately, the women sales reps at EMC report that making family-oriented choices cost them status and, ultimately in some cases, their jobs. One female EMC rep stated that her boss "told her she wasn't qualified to fill a vacant position (on a major account) because she wouldn't smoke, drink, swear, hunt, fish and tolerate strip clubs."[77] All of these are fairly major lifestyle choices this woman made, apparently to her detriment.

Retention

Women chief sales executives describe innovations to help their companies keep valuable female talent from wanting to look for greener pastures, based in large part on their own experiences.

Nancy Sells, of PR Newswire Association, revised her sales processes to fit the flexibility her female sales stars required, rather than lose them. "We redesigned our process into inside and outside sales," she explains. "Inside sales reps work out of their homes. We provide them the latest in technology and tools that promote productivity. These reps have just as many customers and just as big a book of business as

---

[76] Bulkeley, A1.

[77] Bulkeley, A1.

outside sales reps who work in the office and on the road—the more traditional sales approach.

"Although we never make a female vs. male distinction for this job, over time the sales force has become predominantly women. Inside positions that started out being viewed as not quite as good as the outside positions are now the coveted positions. This redesign has turned into one of our best retention tools and has increased productivity enormously." Women who choose to take time out of the work force find that the company welcomes them back and encourages them to return when it suits the woman's lifestyle needs. Says Sells, "We always leave the door open for women who want to come back."

That approach resonates well with Millennial women. As an executive, after you have convinced these young, high-potential sales women to stay on the job, your next challenge may be how to keep these "can do" workers on track even when promotions do not open up overnight.

That kind of fast track may seem like an absurd expectation, but it is just one of many distinguishing beliefs held by the younger crowd. They feel their opinion counts, regardless of seniority, and should be seriously considered, whereas prior generations hesitated to speak up in a group of more seasoned colleagues. If they did venture an opinion, it was usually with a lack of confidence in its worthiness. Another differentiating belief held by many of today's incoming young employees is that if they work hard, they will get promoted as a foregone consequence—that may sound very familiar to Baby Boomers. If a Millennial performs a job well, the instant gratification of either promotion or greatly increased responsibility is expected, regardless of how new that employee may be to the position. It may take some serious negotiating to convince a top performer that she is not yet ready for the next job.

The good news, says Jocelyn Talbot, of RetirementJobs.com, is that these young women want to be successful. They may define success differently than do the Baby Boomers, but they want to succeed. Money and flexibility that come with attaining titles and moving up the career ladder are important to the lifestyle for which they strive.

The Long Haul

A key to keeping these young women motivated for the long climb up the ladder is consistency from hiring to training to measuring and feedback. This generation grew up in an instant feedback world. They are used to being stimulated via multiple and simultaneous inputs. They learn fast and process data quickly from various streams and sources. They can read electronic messages and accurately interpret emotions from what may seem to their Baby Boomer elders an incomprehensible stream of characters and symbols. Text messaging at every opportunity, they maintain continuous contact with their colleagues, friends and family throughout the day. From cell phones to iPods to blogs to social applications such as Facebook, LinkedIn and Twitter, the emerging generation of business professionals reaches out for information, and they want it now, and non-stop.

On the job, this plugged-in posture enables them to readily spot insincerity or avoidance in relationships. They need to hear a consistent message from the boss beginning with the hiring process, through the initial "honeymoon" period, and continuing into the various career stages of their tenure with the company.

These young workers want to know clearly what is expected of them, how it will be measured, and that the boss will be consistent in that measurement. They accept the task of deciding if the journey is worth the investment. If the boss is clear up front, neither party will be surprised. If the hiring manager does not clearly lay out the role, performance measures, work approach and habits, as well as the likely next steps and reasonable time frames, they will make their own assumptions. Friction is likely to result if those assumptions do not align well with the expectations of those in charge—the older generation.

Whether delivered to the young and maturing saleswoman by the boss, a mentor, a coach or a peer, it will be critical to debrief often and consistently in order to glean nuggets from what might seem to be the ordinary tasks of the sales rep's day. Both sides should have a clear vision of what is expected, as well as be able to articulate the steps that should be taken to arrive at short-term and long-term goals. One method to consider is establishing a buddy system or mentoring program, pairing older women to younger women, even if that woman is not the boss, so that the message being given is consistent from day to day and across behaviors and experiences. The Millennials aspiring to high achievement in sales already know there is a lot of competition, so the goal is to help them set reasonable job and career expectations and keep them motivated and intent on reaching the targets, thus deepening the pool of competent and experienced female applicants for those future leadership openings.

CHAPTER 14

Convergence

Business realities. Lifestyle choices. Chief sales executives. Gender bias. Millennials. Baby Boomers. Generation X. Strengths. Talents. Mentors. Role models. Women. Men. Families. Leadership. Relationships. Hiring. Retiring. Promotions. Competition. Tradition. Change.

These elements and more comprise a living collage of today's competitive business world, a cacophony of attitudes, tradition, trends, desires, fears and purposes. It all seems very confusing if we look too closely. But, if we stand back the picture becomes quite clear: The business world is operating with half a mind and one-third of a heart. Decision-makers continue to slam the door in the face of women at the very time their companies need all the leadership talent they can muster, especially in the revenue-generating sales arena. Organizations that plod along in the rut of male bias intentionally forfeit the strengths that women offer—50 percent of the nation's stockpile of intelligence and about 67 percent of the nurturing intuition.

How smart is that?

Job requirements for sales leadership continue to evolve and broaden, raising the bar for success higher and wider. Achieving sales performance metrics, traditionally dominated by men, no longer guarantees success. The future belongs to sales leaders who not only make the numbers and satisfy customers, but who possess the typically identified female strengths to develop, engage and support the diverse lifestyle needs of their salespeople.

The senior global sales executive at the IT firm elaborates on that point. "Many of my male peers are very intellectual, extremely good at the engineering approach, organizing, taking things apart and putting them together," she notes. "But, attributes that tend to be inherent in females, perhaps more than males, are caring and nurturing and wanting life to be better for everybody who is in your care. If my sellers struggle because I haven't thought through something, or I ask them to do something I can't do myself, or I do not empathize with their situation in the marketplace, or I have sales leaders who cannot find opportunities to grow their careers, those are the problems I feel driven to solve every day when I come to work."

In a similar vein, Georgia Power Company's Anne Kaiser widened the scope of her leadership role with positive results. When she took over as vice president of sales, Kaiser found a loose sales structure and little emphasis on tracking progress with statistics. She quickly restructured the organization and added the discipline of tracking each group's contribution against numeric goals. "It surprised everyone that I came in and ran the organization like a man, when the man had not!" Kaiser recalls.

Georgia Power salespeople—primarily male engineers with an average of 27 years' tenure—spend only one-half of their time on direct sales. Kaiser carefully segmented the markets and products to determine the contribution each makes to the overall corporation. This structure and additional discipline earned her credibility as an outsider who understood the business, even though she did not grow up "stringing line between poles."

With her prior experience at accounting and legal firms, Kaiser says, "I know how to speak using data, in very linear terms. I understand that sales is a numbers and data game. But I also know how to motivate, inspire and play to the emotional characteristics of my sales force."

Keeping the Door Open

Just as spring follows winter, younger workers will replace the older ones in any organization over time. As Millennial workers bring their innate acceptance of diverse people, beliefs and lifestyles into a company, traditional views of what career women should and should not do begin to fade away. They want the door to success to stay open. They see lifestyles and careers with new eyes.

When they enter the life phase of parenthood, the younger generation will more fully embrace the trend, which began in the last decade with the Generation Xers, of deciding whether the woman or man is best suited to stay at home with the kids while the other parent brings home the bacon. They will not hesitate to explore all options and choose the one best suited to their situation. Today, the choice by dads to stay at home is more accepted than even just a few years ago, and the numbers of parents making this choice are continuing to grow. According to a U.S. Census Bureau report, in 2003 there were 98,000 stay-at-home dads out of a total of 5.5 million stay-at-home parents. Merely one and one-half years later, by May of 2005, there were 143,000 stay-at-home dads and 5.6

million stay-at-home moms.[78] As parents, Millennials may well adopt more holistic lifestyle attitudes, with more freedom than their parents perceived they had to choose their familial roles.

Ironically, the advancement of Millennial workers into leadership arenas may strengthen what was once perceived to be a more traditional female role. After all, what is so different about a young person wanting a life that incorporates family, fun, work and service to humanity in a holistic way, and a woman asking for a season to be available for story time at her child's school, or to volunteer or travel as a family before the children graduate and go off on their own?

Studies by Hewitt Associates show little difference between the views of men and women 20 to 28 years old about work-life balance.[79] It is only older workers, especially those age 40 and over, who feel they have hit road blocks or have had to downsize their ambitions—a concept Millennials do not easily grasp. Their view starts off with a healthy, but holistic, set of ambitions in life and career.

New Attitudes

Partly because many of them watched their Baby Boomer, success-focused parents end up in divorce court, Millennial youth seek to avoid that same outcome through more balance in work and life. They often wait until later in life to marry, have children and begin a nest egg. They will accept a lower salary if that will keep their weekends free.

Indeed, all workers rate flexibility and time off as an expectation, as part of the job benefits. But younger workers view time off to

---

[78] U.S. Bureau of the Census, November 2004, and May 2006.

[79] Hewitt Associates, "Hot Topics in Sales Management and Sales Compensation," 2001.

He Saw Potential in Me

JOCELYN TALBOT
Vice President, Sales
RetirementJobs.com
(formerly Senior Vice President, Sales, Monster.com)

While a young rep and as a first-time sales manager at Wang, Talbot learned from a boss who came from IBM, her company's arch rival, and who was a product of IBM's excellent training program of the 70s.

When a new sales rep joined the company, the boss always sent a bottle of champagne home with the rep. At the end of each year, he wrote a letter to the family of each sales rep thanking them for their support and contribution throughout the year. He knew his reps could not do the job without the understanding and support at home.

"I saw the impact that had on both the reps and their families," recalls Talbot." I copied this leader's style as I grew up in management. He saw potential in me that I did not. But he showed his confidence in me and after my first management job, it got easier."

travel or do things that bring them personal fulfillment as a primary component of their benefits package during their search for a job. Young workers with children need flexibility to raise their children and deal with health and education issues. Conversely, older workers need flexibility to care for aging parents. The fresh attitude of the incoming employees may therefore be a boon to the older employees as well, who desire the same flexibility in their work life but have not demanded it as fervently. All may benefit from the winds of change the Millennials stir up as they enter the work force.

The new views about careers and lifestyles are rapidly being embraced by the general population, primarily due to the increasingly ubiquitous nature of social communication. Advancing technologies are pushing messages, music, visuals and concepts through the cultural pipeline faster and more directly than any past generation could imagine. The unexpected result will be a gradual melding of Baby Boomer and Millennial cultures. That generational melding may be accelerated by the technology specific to this new generation.

Even though Generations X and Y created the iPod phenomenon, today Baby Boomer women top the list of raving iPod adopters. According to a Solutions Research Group study, women in the 30 to 49 age category showed the highest increase in iPod downloads over any other segment during 2005-2006.[80] Baby Boomer music is coming back around. Baby Boomer musicians and songs are now popular with the Millennial demographic.

It is clear that both generations have a passion for gadgets. Could iPods be another connection between Baby Boomers and Millennials? Both groups seek to become more efficient and connected. Why cannot fun, fast-paced lessons from the older set be fashioned into clusters of short messages—"Podcasts from the Priors?"

Facebook, another social communication phenomenon, started in 2004 as an application to connect college students and to help them share knowledge across disciplines and campuses. It quickly took on a life of its own and users have turned it into a social communication network. Already, 40 percent of Facebook's users are adults, albeit a percentage of those use it to monitor their teenagers' postings. But legitimate adult usage continues to increase, and by the end of 2007, less than 30 percent of Facebook's users were college students.[81] Facebook's brilliant young founder, Mark Zuckerberg, saw the expanded potential

---

[80] Peter Cohen, Study: "iPod use tripled in women in 2006," *Playlist*, July 13, 2006, Solutions Research Group.

[81] Steven Levy, "Facebook Grows Up," *Newsweek Magazine*, August 27, 2007, 42.

of his creation and opened up its technology for everyone to design applications, making it ideal for older and younger generations to share professional learning, tips and techniques.

As the powerful explosion of our society's ability to share views and information continues to reverberate, we must be ever more mindful of our responsibility to send the right messages in the right ways, and to develop the attitudes, as well as the skills, of the next generation of workers and sales leaders.

In Search of Balance

At the end of the day, our interviews hint that business, demographics and social forces are poised to accelerate the advancement of women to senior leadership positions in sales and other disciplines. Successful female chief sales executives, in particular, will be those who balance their natural strengths with business imperatives.

Colleen Honan, of OneSource, advises aspiring sales professionals and leaders to aim for achieving job satisfaction while at the same time building their professional expertise and reputation. "What I love most about working with Millennials is that they want to have satisfying careers that support a successful life," Honan says. "In short, they plan to make work-life balance a reality. However, while they believe that 'what you do' shouldn't define you as a person, the fact is that 'how you do it' does."

Although as we have demonstrated, women tend to lead by nurturing and men seem pre-disposed to lead based on numbers, neither gender has a lock on those attributes. Some men do succeed using people skills and some women excel at the numbers game—a perfect convergence of numbers and nurture. "In my industry of entertainment marketing, the men say they can't be bothered by the calculations," says Karen Bressner, of TiVo. "But I believe that behind every strong male chief sales officer, there is a woman crunching the numbers!"

Bressner claims that her affinity for numbers blossomed at the Craps table, a secret she reveals to potential employers and employees. "I almost always try to bring this into the interview conversation," she confides. "The response tells me a lot about that person's comfort with numbers, odds and risk. If a candidate walked in with all the right track record and loved to play Craps, I would want to hire that person! Math is a very important skill set."

Acknowledging and intentionally strengthening one's own combination of male and female traits also leads to a more balanced lifestyle, contends Rebecca Bernson, of ADP. She learned that to show both your male numbers side and female nurturing side requires abundant self-confidence and the ability to stay in touch with who you are.

"Most men do not display the female relational and nurturing traits, because they are not in touch as much with their female side," she says. "Men see relationships taking up their time, 'Hey, I have numbers to make; I don't have time to do the relationship thing.'"

Bernson took a new approach to motivate a group of male reps to sell up to plan and make the numbers. "I told them that life is not equal to your sales plan, that life encompasses a lot of things outside of this company," she recalls. "I said to them, 'The answer to making your numbers this year is probably not to work harder. Do not measure yourself just by the percent of quota. Take a look at your life and where you are. You have to have a life, guys, and it is not just all about work.'" That message inspired the reps, she notes. "It rang true to who I was, and those people who had worked for me for years knew I really meant it."

No Limits to Success

DORANE WINTERMEYER
Vice President, Sales
Regence Blue Cross Blue Shield of Oregon

Wintermeyer gives her whole family credit as early and critical role models. She grew up in a "fully functional family" on a farm. The farm gave her the work ethic that she does not see in the typical person she encounters on a daily basis. It was hard work and long hours, from dawn to dusk—not that dissimilar to what it has taken to achieve the career she has built for herself.

Farm life also taught Wintermeyer self-esteem. Careers, like farm work, "require a sense of ego and cocky self-confidence that you can accomplish something regardless of the hurdles."

Asked who most helped her get to where she is today, she replied without a pause, "I had an incredible math teacher who taught in very creative ways that a traditional math teacher would not use, but he taught us there were no gender barriers and no limits to our opportunities for success."

Dorane Wintermeyer, of Regence Blue Cross Blue Shield of Oregon, echoes the sentiment that neither gender can be pigeonholed. "Succeeding includes not only knowing career goals, but also having real personal fun goals, and a continual attitude about learning," she says. "There are things that cause me to be successful because I am goal-oriented at work and in my personal life. I climb mountains, and my goal is to climb all fifty-five 14,000-foot peaks in Colorado. I also have other areas that I'm heavily invested in, such as giving back to the community. It's not just success at work, it's success in lots of areas. I don't think that is gender-specific. I find this position in male counterparts as well. So, success to me means being balanced."

The good news is that success comes in many packages—female and male, young and old. Each woman has the opportunity to define her success, building on the knowledge and experience of her corporate ancestors, as well as her own knowledge of her innate strengths and abilities. How she chooses to blend the two ultimately will determine the uppermost rung she attains on the ladder of sales success and the mark she leaves once she gets there.

Epilogue

After all the interviews and research, only a small portion of which made it to the pages of this book, the author remains convinced that, more than ever, this is an important time for women in executive leadership. And, because driving revenue is often a critical success factor of a company, sales is perhaps the most visible place to start to show the world the benefits of having the right woman in the top executive sales leadership role.

So can we chat? Let's leave behind the sometimes stilted third-person format and talk person to person.

I have now been a CEO four times. On the way to becoming a CEO, I held positions in marketing, sales, services and operations. I have started companies and sold companies. I have been a C-level leader in small and large organizations, both private and public. I have served on the boards of growth companies and troubled companies. I have seen the good, the bad and the ugly of the business landscape. Like most of the women in our study, along the way, I have had few female peers. Those I have had are often people I am still in touch with on some basis of frequency. Whereas, earlier in our careers we stuck together for strength and safety, today we band together in mentoring and coaching the next generation. We, like the generation of women before us, hope that our efforts will mean a different world for the young women entering sales or any other professional career today.

In the process of identifying and researching candidates for this study, and subsequently interviewing them and compiling the data, I met some outstanding women and learned from all of them. Most have gone much further up the sales ladder than I ever chose to go. All of us have had failures more numerous than our successes. But we have each become adept at learning from each other, from the bad as well as the good experiences. As we have gotten older, I think we have also learned to be more transparent about those failures and successes and have found greater insight in that transparency.

As I write this final chapter, our global economy is tight, consumer confidence is low and jobs are disappearing. Funny thing about sales jobs—they are always in demand. Good salespeople are the ones who drive the revenue necessary to dig us out of our economic woes. Strong revenues drive jobs and jobs drive economic recovery and consumer confidence.

So why do I have such confidence in women sales leaders around the globe? The women in our study give me this great confidence.

1. **Women are can-do people. Women stick with the job and get it done.** Eighty-six percent of the women in our study climbed to the chief sales executive position in the same company in which they began their career. They may have eventually gone on to this position in other companies, but they demonstrated a "stick-to-it-ive-ness" that men generally do not. It takes women much longer to reach the

top position, but once they do, women stay in the chief sales positions much longer than do men. Sometimes it takes a long time to turn an organization into a selling machine. If the leader changes during any long-term venture, progress is slowed or never truly made. If the organization is in trouble, it may never recover without consistent, nurturing, sure leadership—the ship sinks if the captain jumps ship before the job is done.

2. **Women have extraordinary capacity to multitask. They juggle many roles without slighting any of them.** The myth that women can be successful at work or at home, but not both, has been totally shattered by the competent women we interviewed. In fact, women today spend about the same amount of time on family activities as did women of 25 years ago. All but one of our interviewees, who is single, have long-term marriages, supportive husbands who partner with them in raising the children and caring for the home, and smart, active and engaged children who are gaining first-hand knowledge that women are successful business people. Most women do seem to have the innate ability to multi-task and rapidly adjust priorities. Our interviewees found ways to create greater flexibility in how, when and where the job gets done to allow them to better juggle their various life responsibilities. In the process, they improved their respective companies by decreasing turnover, increasing team productivity, and retaining people who love their jobs. Everyone wins.

3. **Women balance the numbers and the people equation. Women know the numbers count, but so do the names behind the numbers.** More than just the names, these women take the time to know their people and understand the culture of the team and what it takes to succeed. The numbers tell the end result, but by then it is too late to change what it took to get to the result. Numbers are yesterday's news and tomorrow's troubles. It is critical to set goals, measure as we go and celebrate at the end of the race. But people are not numbers and the next generation, perhaps more than any before it, does not want to be a number. They want adventure to be part of their daily lives, not just an experience merely reserved for vacation time or postponed until a dim, distant retirement.

4. **Women understand the tribal nature of raising the next generation—men or women.** Just like economic recovery, grooming the next generation takes time, talent and touch. It means being intentional about passing on the experiences of the decades-long climb to the top. It means making mentoring a priority, not just a "when it is convenient" or "when I have time" investment. Women understand that driving performance is more than managing to the numbers for short-term gain. Intentional investment in mentoring, training, flexible job design, and building teams—not merely focusing on individual performers and nine-to-five schedules—prepares the next generation to confidently take the reins. Despite the time it may take away from what others might see as the immediate tasks of making quota or

fast-tracking the climb up the career ladder, the women who lead today's sales organizations realize the critical role they play in preparing the next generation to lead in a way many of them have only dreamed of leading or being led.

Despite the obstacles the women in our study faced in their careers, they demonstrated clearly that the rewards are there for the women who have the appetite, energy and sheer will to succeed. But it takes having a plan, setting goals, creating accountability to those goals, plus the right support along the way—bosses, mentors, peers, husbands or other family—to make attaining the pinnacle a reality.

The women in our study are real, vibrant and true role models for women everywhere. They are building successful sales organizations while they intentionally invest in young women inside their companies, their communities and their families. They are also investing in young men, never forgetting that it takes both genders to build strong companies, countries and families.

Summary

There is still work for both men and women to do on behalf of bright women seeking to maximize their God-given talents, and on behalf of organizations everywhere who may unknowingly be wasting up to half of their talent pool by not helping these women achieve their best. The good news is that we live in a day of brightly visible women role models. Regardless of one's political affinity, there is no doubt that the United States of the early 21st century demonstrates to the world that it is a country where women can be strong, recognized and respected leaders. Whether one looks at a presidential race or to the House of Representatives or the Cabinet, women are front and center.

They are influential and demonstrate polished sales skills or they would never have reached the levels they have attained. As one of our interviewees mused, "Every job the rest of your life requires you to be a good salesperson." How true.

Challenge

If you are a woman in sales aspiring to be an executive in sales leadership, I hope this book will encourage and equip you for the journey ahead. If you are a hiring manager, man or woman, sales or human resources, working with the line manager, I hope this book will help you make sound decisions about the people you hire and those you strive to grow and retain. If you are already the top dog, your role as CEO is even more important because the culture of the organization is set at the top. I hope the messages from these executive sales women, who often report to you and who clearly drive your revenue, will inspire you to find ways for the culture to flow—not just trickle—down through the organization for the gain of everyone inside and outside the company.

The counsel of the women in this book applies to any woman (or man!) seeking to climb the ladder of corporate success. Whether you are in sales or some other function, profit or not-for-profit, public or private, let the messages of these women guide and encourage you.

It is time for all of us in positions of leadership to pay serious attention to the other half of our work force. We all have something to learn from each other and this is the way tribal knowledge has always been created and shared—one person at a time caring enough to pass the torch, formally and informally. We have received the hand-off and must shoulder the responsibility of keeping the flame alight.

Well, I must run to my next meeting, as I know you must also! Let's continue the dialogue. To carry on the progress of our bold female forebearers, join the tribe on our blog at www.womanontopbook.com. Make your own contribution to the body of tribal knowledge. Share your experiences as a head of sales (or any other function) or as one who aspires to the role. Please also share your feedback on the findings of this study and keep the torch glowing!

Acknowledgements

At the risk of yet another syrupy ode to motherhood, as you will shortly learn, my mother never spent a day of her life in sales, or even in business, yet she tops the list of women who have shaped my life and my career. To this day, after more than 35 years of periodic discussions about my career, she could not really tell you what I do for a living. She has never truly forgiven me for not being a scientist or a mathematician and delights in reminding me that I could have been a good one. I am, in turn, delighted by that simple statement.

You see, that declaration is an accolade coming from my mother, who earned a Ph.D. in physical chemistry at the tender age of 26. She did that in her "spare time" between her responsibilities as a wife and mother of three demanding young children. A fourth child would come along after she was well established in her full-time career as a university professor and additional jobs as president of the faculty, city councilwoman, Girl Scout and Cub Scout leader, and deacon and head of the finance committee at church—to name only a few of her many roles. Although now retired from the university for several years, she remains quite active in volunteer activities, teaching and church work.

While protesting that business was alien to her and even the very word had an evil ring, she skillfully led, managed, mentored, coached and established records like any other successful businesswoman. She set the bar for my sister and me at a lofty height the two of us are still aspiring to reach and influenced the tone of our attitudes toward females in the professional world. Oh, that women sales leaders today could have at least one such role model! So, I thank my mother, Dr. Charlotte Ward, for her many years of investing in me, mentoring me and preparing me for the world of business.

Closer in time, this book would never have happened without the major support of three other people who invested extraordinary time and heroic effort to see it through from inception to publication.

Laura Jesseph, who has been my faithful, dependable, responsible, inspirational and fun sidekick for ten years, was at the restaurant table when the idea was birthed for a book that would capture and pass along the lessons I have learned in my 30-plus years in business. Laura never let me forget the dream and cracked the whip daily for the two years of interviewing, writing and editing it took to make the vision a reality. She managed all the details of publishing a book and left me to do the writing. She read the manuscript, proofed it several times and developed the book's marketing plan. To say I could never have completed this effort without Laura would be a huge understatement. I am grateful for her incredible work ethic and her enormously high level of productivity even while managing the lives of preschool twin girls, a traveling husband and our core consulting business. Just as critical to our partnership is Laura's ability to laugh both at me and with me when that is truly the only thing to do. Laura is a dear friend and colleague.

David Henry has been a friend and associate since Laura and I first met him on a client assignment in 2003. David is a talented, professional communicator and speech writer who has been the man behind the words of high level executives in household-name companies such as The Home Depot and The Coca-Cola Company. Halfway through the project, our quantitative research team dropped out of the project and created a go/no go juncture. It was David who offered to take the chapters already written to support the anticipated data, plus stacks and stacks of raw interview data, and turn the jumble into a viable manuscript that could stand alone as a purely qualitative work. He accurately captured my voice as he wove together my raw manuscript and the remaining interview data I had not yet incorporated. David took me to the point of being able to see that a book really did exist in the many disparate pages I had created to that point.

Lastly, only because she got stuck with clean-up detail, is Marta Ward, my talented and long suffering sister-in-law, whose skills as a proofreader and editor have truly been life-saving for this manuscript. Marta's ability to spot a dangling participle, a stray split infinitive or a mismatched subject and verb is super human. Her keen eye for nonsense logic, missing arguments and extraneous text has made the book much more readable and valuable. Marta has given up many evenings and weekends and time with my brother to proof and edit this manuscript. I am grateful for her patience with me and for her extraordinary attention to detail and perfection. Most of all, I am grateful to still count Marta as a friend as well as family. There were many times, especially as we labored late into the night after a full day at work, that she could have disowned me, but did not even grumble.

While these three people invested heavily in the creation of this book, there are others I would be remiss in not acknowledging and publicly thanking. I am grateful to Greg Alexander, co-author of *Making the Number: How to Use Sales Benchmarking to Drive*

Performance and *Topgrading for Sales: How to Interview, Hire, and Coach Top Sales Representatives*, for suggesting the idea that moved our original *Lessons Learned* book concept to the focus on women sales leaders. I am also grateful to Clarke Bishop for re-introducing me to Greg and for his many hours of brainstorming the marketing and distribution of the book. My deep appreciation goes to Daryl Toor for his valuable input, from his participation at the original lunch where the *Lessons Learned* concept was birthed to his ongoing investment in the public relations potential of the book. And I am very grateful to Brynne Ward, my talented young niece, who did hours of tedious Internet research for the book and represented the critical eye of the rising Millennial generation of businesswomen. She read through the manuscript at least twice in its entirety and offered cogent comments and unique perspectives I otherwise might have missed.

Last, but most certainly, not least, I am thankful for my husband who has been my greatest fan, encourager and critic since we were 17 years old. Who else would sense the discouragement in his young wife's voice after the only other two women bailed out of her IBM sales school and drive four hours after a full day's work to encourage her for two hours to "hang in there," then turn around and drive back home to do the night shift for a sick employee? Yes, John Morris has been my number one partner in school, work, play, ministry and life for almost four decades. I pray we have many more decades of fun, health and significant endeavors together, the good Lord willing.

Selected Bibliography by Chapter

Listed here are not only many of the sources that were of use in creating the book, but also a sampling of the wide range of other sources that are available for additional reading. This bibliography is by no means a complete record of every source that was consulted, or of all that is available on each topic. The list is intended as a resource for those who wish to pursue additional reading related to the subject matter in each chapter. For ease of reference, the sources are listed by chapter.

Chapter 1 – Introduction

Business and Professional Women's Foundation. "101 Facts on the Status of Workingwomen" (October 2007).

U.S. Department of Labor, Bureau of Labor Statistics, Employment and Earnings. *2006 Annual Averages and the Monthly Labor Review.* http://www.dol.gov/wb/stats/main.htm (accessed October 10, 2007); 2007 Center for Women's Business Research. http://cfwbr. org/facts/index.php (accessed October 10, 2007).

Chapter 2 – My Story

Bulkeley, William M. "Tech and Testosterone: A Data-Storage Titan Confronts Bias Claims." *Wall Street Journal* (September 12, 2007).

Facts and Figures. "Mothers at Work." Economic Policy Institute. http://www.epi. org/newsroom/releases/2005/05/05050_Mothers_Day_Facts.pdf.

Greenberg, Quinlan, Rosner and Polimetrix. *Coming of Age in America, Part II.* Washington, DC, 2005.

Section One – Tomorrow is Here

Chapter 3 – Welcome to the Real World

Business and Professional Women's Foundation. "101 Facts on the Status of Workingwomen" (October 2007).

Cook, Ellen P., Mary J. Heppner and Karen M. O'Brien. "Career development of women of color and White women: assumptions, conceptualization, and interventions from an ecological perspective - Special Section." *Career Development Quarterly* (June 2002).

Lyness, K.S. and C.A. Schrader. "Moving Ahead or Just Moving? An Examination of Gender Differences in Senior Corporate Management Appointments." *Group Organization Management*, 2006. 651-676. http://gom.sagepub.com/cgi/content/refs/ 31/6/651.

Sales Benchmark Index. "World Class 100 Report." Survey of 3,700 U.S. publicly traded companies across 19 industries from 1996-2006.

Sloan Work and Family Research Network. *Fact Sheet.* "Questions and Answers about Women in the Workforce." Boston College. http://wfnetwork.bc.edu/pdfs/womenwork.pdf, updated June 2008.

U.S. Department of Labor, Bureau of Labor Statistics, Employment and Earnings. *2006 Annual Averages and the Monthly Labor Review.* http://www.dol.gov/wb/stats/main.htm (accessed October 10, 2007); 2007 Center for Women's Business Research. http://cfwbr. org/facts/index.php (accessed October 10, 2007).

Weisman, Robert. "Shifting Stars." Harvard study suggesting female executives outperform males when taking a new job. *The Boston Globe* (March 30, 2008). http://www.boston.com/business/articles/2008/03/30/shifting_stars/.

Chapter 4 – Lifestyles

American Business Collaboration. "Generation & Gender in the Workplace." Families and Work Institute, Watertown, MA, 2004. http://www.familiesandwork. org/announce/ 2002NSCW.html.

Bond, J.T., C. Thompson, E. Galinsky and D. Prottas. "Highlights of the national study of the changing workforce." Families and Work Institute, NewYork, NY. 2002. http://www. familiesandwork.org/announce/2002NSCW.html.

Boushey, H. "Are women opting out? Debunking the myth." Washington, DC Center for Economic and Policy Research. 2005, 11. http://www.cepr.net/ publications/opt_out_ 2005_11.pdf (accessed January 28, 2006).

Christianity Today. "The Fatherless Child" (October 2007): 25. Citing Pew Study, www.pewresearch.org/assets/social/pdf/marriage.pdf.

Connelly, R. and J. Kimmel. "Marital Status and full-time/part-time work status in child care choices." *Applied Economics* 35(7) (2003): 761-777.

Dieringer Research Group. "WorldatWork 2006 Telework Trendlines™ Survey." Summarized and edited online by Katie Hoynski, The Telework Advisory Group of WorldatWork, Fall 2006 University of Wisconsin-Eau Claire *Working.* http://www. workingfromanywhere.org.

DiNatale, M. and S. Boraas. "The Labor Force Experience of Women from 'Generation X.'" *Monthly Labor Review* 125(3) (2002): 3-15. http://www.bls.gov/ cps/home.htm.

Galinsky, E. and J.T. Bond. *Business work-life study: A sourcebook.* Families and Work Institute, New York, NY. 1998. http://www.familiesandwork.org/index. asp?PageAction= VIEWPROD&ProdID=9.

Hewlett, Sylvia Ann. "Off-Ramps and On-Ramps." Interview by Melinda Morino during *Harvard Business Review* podcast, May 24, 2007. Also in "Sylvia Hewlett on Helping Women Succeed." *WFC* Resources (June 2007).

Knowles, John. "Why Are Married Men Working So Much? The Macroeconomics of Bargaining Between Spouses." *IZA Discussion Papers*. University of Pennsylvania and Institute for the Study of Labor (IZA). No. 2909, revised February 2008.

MetLife Mature Market Institute & National Alliance for Caregiving. "MetLife caregiving cost study: productivity losses to U.S. business." Westport, CT, 2006. http://www. pascenter.org/frames/pas_frame.php?site=http%3A%2F%2Fwww. caregiving.org%2F pubs%2Fdata.htm (accessed April 25, 2007).

Shackelford, Monisa, Ph.D. "Generation X Professional Women Leaving the Workforce to Become Full-time, Stay-at-home Mothers: A Qualitative Analysis of Motivation, Meaning, and Mindful Parenting." Louisiana State University.

Sloan Work and Family Research Network. "Eldercare at the Workplace." Boston College. http://wfnetwork.bc.edu/pdfs/ElderCare.pdf.

Chapter 5 – Baby Boomers Engaging Millennials

Benavides, Dr. Lily. Executive Summary, Doctoral Study: The Impact of Executive Coaching on the Organizational Performance of Female Executives. University of San Francisco, February 24, 2009.

Borden, Lisa. "Next Gen Wants You." *Discipleship Journal* 159, NavPress® (May/June 2007): 46.

Coupland, Douglas. *Generation X: Tales for an Accelerated Culture*. St. Martin's Press, New York, NY, 1991.

Cray, Dan, Tom Curry, and William McWhirter. "Twentysomething." *Time* (July 16, 1990).

He, Wan, Manisha Sengupta, Victoria A. Velkoff and Kimberly A. DeBarros. "65+ in the United States: 2005." National Institute on Aging, U.S. Census Bureau.

Hira, Nadira A. "Attracting the Twentysomething Worker." *Fortune*, May 28, 2007.

Howe, Neil and William Strauss. *Millennials Rising: The Next Great Generation*. Vintage Books, New York, NY, 2000.

Howe, Neil and William Strauss. "The Next 20 Years: How Customer and Workforce Attitudes Will Evolve." *Harvard Business Review* (July-August 2007): 41-52.

Koster, Kelly and Alexandra Smith. "From Workplace to Marketplace: How Millennial work values translate into brand opportunity." Inconoculture. July 2007 blog.

RoperASW. "Baby Boomers Envision Retirement II - Key Findings, Survey of Baby Boomers' Expectations for Retirement." Prepared for AARP. Copyright 2004, AARP, Knowledge Management, 601 E. Street, NW, Washington, DC 20049. http://research. aarp.org.

Stamp, Mary. "Students Today Accept Traditional Beliefs." *The Fig Tree*. Washington State University (March 3, 2006). http://www.thefigtree.org/march06/stearns.html.

Sweeney, Richard. "Millennial Behaviors & Demographics." New Jersey Institute of Technology. University Heights, Newark, NJ 07102-1982. Revised December 22, 2006.

Chapter 6 – The Road Ahead

Bauerlein, Mark. "The Dumbest Generation: How the Digital Age Stupifies Young Americans and Jeopardizes Our Future (Or Don't Trust Anyone under 30)." 2007.

Berrens, Camilla. "Generation X." *New Statesman and Society* vol. 7-8 (February 3, 1995): 22-23.

Business and Professional Women's Foundation. "101 Facts on the Status of Workingwomen." October 2007.

Coupland, Douglas. *Generation X: Tales for an Accelerated Culture*. St. Martin's Press, New York, NY, 1991.

Gravett, Linda, Ph.D, SPHR. "Building a Bridge Across Generations." e-HResources.com. http://www.e-hresources.com/Articles/Sept1.htm.

Gross, David M. and Sophronia Scott. "Proceeding With Caution." *Time* (Monday, July 16, 1990).

Healy, Ryan. "Generation Y - 10 Ways Generation Y Will Change the Workplace." *Work/Life* (May 23, 2008).

Kart, Suzanne. "Gen X Women: We Need to Mentor our Millennial Sisters." *GenerationXpert* blog. April 15, 2008. http://genxpert.blogspot.com.

Lancaster, L. C. and D. Stillman. *When Generations Collide*. Harper Collins, New York, 2002.

Martin, C. A., and B. Tulgan. *Managing Generation Y*. HRD Press, Amherst, MA, 2001.

McCraw, Thomas. *Prophet of Innovation: Joseph Schumpeter and Creative Destruction*. Belknap Press of Harvard University Press, 2007.

Mencimer, Stephanie. "The Baby Boycott – Decline in birth rates attributed in part to Family Leave Act." *The Washington Monthly* (June 2001).

Oblinger, D. "Boomers, Gen-Xers, & Millennials: Understanding the New Students." *EDUCUSE Review* (July/August 2003).

Prensky, M. "Digital Natives-Digital Immigrants." *On the Horizon* vol. 9 no. 5, NCB University Press, (October 2001).

Ritchie, Karen. "Sophisticated, Cynical, and 'Surfing." *American Demographics* vol. 17, no. 6 (June, 1995).

Seligson, Hannah. "Damsels in Success." Blog. http://www.damselsinsuccess.com/blogs/blog.aspx?id=86.

Trunk, Penelope. "What Gen Y Really Wants." *Time* (Thursday, July 05, 2007). http://www.time.com/time/magazine/article/0,9171,1640395,00.html.

U.S. Department of Labor, Bureau of Labor Statistics, Employment and Earnings. *2006 Annual Averages and the Monthly Labor Review*. http://www.dol.gov/wb/stats/main.htm (accessed October 10, 2007); 2007 Center for Women's Business Research. http://cfwbr. org/facts/index.php (accessed October 10, 2007).

Zemke, R., C. Raines, and K. Filipcza. *Generations at Work: Managing the Clash of Veterans, Boomers, Xers, and Nexters in Your Workplace*. Amacom, New York, 2000.

Section Two – The Female Strengths

Chapter 7 – Finding Strengths

Cook, Ellen P., Mary J. Heppner and Karen M. O'Brien. "Career development of women of color and White women: assumptions, conceptualization, and interventions from an ecological perspective - Special Section." *Career Development Quarterly*, (June 2002).

Operation SMART is a programmed approach to engaging girls and young women in inquiry-based science, technology, engineering and math through hands-on, minds-on experiences. Developed by: Girls Incorporated® with funding from National Science Foundation, The Ford Foundation, The Carnegie Corporation of New York, The Coca Cola Foundation, CREW Foundation, General Motors Foundation, Verizon Communications, Lucent Technology Foundation, National Endowment for the Humanities and many others.

U.S. Department of Education, National Center for Education Statistics. *Postsecondary Education*, 2002. http://nces.ed.gov/pubs2003/digest02/tables/dt278.asp.

Wyden, Senator Ron. "Title IX and Women in Academics." *Computing Research News* vol. 15, no. 4 (September 2003): 1-8.

Chapter 8 – Nurture vs. Numbers

Bulkeley, William M. "Tech and Testosterone: A Data-Storage Titan Confronts Bias Claims." *Wall Street Journal* (September 12, 2007).

Dillow, Clay. "Numerology: National Boss Day." *FastCompany* no. 129 (October 2008): 42. Copyright 2008 by Mansueto Ventures, LLC, ISSN 1085-9241, New York, NY.

Halvorsen, Rob, Contributing Writer. "Top Sales Careers for Women." *Sales Careers Online*. http://www.salescareersonline.com/articles/article_08022006.html.

Hrehocik, Maureen. "The Best Sales Force: Finding, Keeping, Grooming." October 1, 2007. Citing Greg Alexander, CEO of *Sales Benchmark Index*, in survey of 3,700 U.S. publicly traded companies across 19 industries from 1996-2006.

"Why Women Sell Better." Blog, March 30, 2008. http://blog.inc.com
sold/2008/03/why_women_sell_better_1.html.

Chapter 9 – Purpose and Passion

Hrehocik, Maureen. "The Best Sales Force: Finding, Keeping, Grooming." October
1, 2007. Citing Greg Alexander, CEO of *Sales Benchmark Index*, in survey of 3,700
U.S. publicly traded companies across 19 industries from 1996-2006.

Chapter 10 – Leadership

Eagly, Alice H. and Linda L. Carli. "Women and the Labyrinth of Leadership."
Harvard Business Review (September 2007).

Ruderman, Marian. "Leadership Lessons: Next Steps for High-Achieving Women."
Center for Creative Leadership. 2007.

ZoomInfo. "ZoomInfo InSite Report: Gender in the Executive Suite. A Quantitative
View of Gender roles in Business Leadership." Waltham, MA, June 2007. (www.
zoominfo. com).

Chapter 11 – Intentional Mentoring

Borden, Lisa. "Next Gen Wants You." *Discipleship Journal* 159, NavPress® (May/
June 2007): 44-49.

Business Wire. "Mentors of Women, by Women, for Women Growing in
Importance, National Survey Indicates" (February 3, 2003). Cited Catalyst, 1996,
study on women corporate leaders.

Business Wire. "Mentors of Women, by Women, for Women Growing in
Importance, National Survey Indicates" (February 3, 2003). Cited Simmons School
of Management.

Business and Professional Women's Foundation. "101 Facts on the Status of
Workingwomen." October 2007.

Colantuono, Susan L. "Why Mentoring Matters to Women." *Leading Women.* http://www.leadingwomen.biz/displaycommon.cfm?an=1&subarticlenbr=199.

Ericsson, K. Anders, Michael J. Prietula and Edward T. Cokely. "The Making of an Expert." *Harvard Business Review* (July-August 2007): 115-121.

Fels, Anna. "Do Women Lack Ambition?" *Harvard Business Review* (March 2005).

Morris, Betsy. "The New Buddy Act." *Fortune* (October 15, 2007): 76-86.

Offstein, Evan H., Jason Morwick and Amit Shah. "Mentoring programs and jobs: A contingency approach." *Review of Business* (March 22, 2007). http://www. allbusiness. com/management/4508123-1.html.

Pullins, Ellen Bolman, Leslie M. Fine and Wendy L. Warren. "Identifying peer mentors in the sales force: An exploratory investigation of willingness and ability." *Journal of the Academy of Marketing Science,* vol. 24, no. 2 (1996): 125-136.

Society for Industrial and Organizational Psychology (SIOP). "Corporate Mentoring Programs on the Upswing." News release, October 11, 2006. http://www.newswise.com/articles/view/524216/.

Section Three – Making it Happen

Chapter 12 – Passing the Torch of Knowledge

Gupta,Vin, CEO, infoUSA. Omaha, NE. Quoted in *Business Wire* (December 26, 2006).

Hoffmeister, David. The Sales Leadership Center, De Paul University, Chicago. (www.salesleadershipcenter.com). Interview, September 2007.

Infoplease©. "Number of U.S. Colleges and Universities and Degrees Awarded, 2005." 2000–2007 Pearson Education, publishing as Infoplease. October 15, 2008. http://www. infoplease.com/ipa/A0908742.html.

L'Allier, Dr. James J., Ph.D. and Kenneth Kolosh. "Preparing for Baby Boomer Retirement." *CLO Magazine* (2002).

Sales Benchmark Index. Survey of 3,700 U.S. publicly traded companies across 19 industries from 1996-2006.

Svoboda, Elizabeth. "Microsoft Class Action." *Fast Company* (September 2007): 86-95.

Work. "Helicopter Managing Fails With Some Gen-Y & Corporate America's Pushing Back." J.T. August 9, 2007. http://www.employeeevolution.com/ archives/2007/08/09/ helicopter-managing-fails-with-some-gen-y-corporate-americas-pushing-back/.

Chapter 13 – Hiring and Promotion

Bulkeley, William M. "Tech and Testosterone: A Data-Storage Titan Confronts Bias Claims." *Wall Street Journal* (September 12, 2007).

Collins, Jim. *Good to Great.* Chapter 2, 17-40. HarperCollins Publishers Inc., New York, 2001.

Parloff, Roger. "The War Over Unconscious Bias." *Fortune,* vol. 156, no. 8 (October 15, 2007): 90-102.

Chapter 14 – Convergence

Cohen, Peter. "Study: iPod use tripled in women in 2006." *Playlist* (July 13, 2006). Solutions Research Group.

Hewitt Associates. "Hot Topics in Sales Management and Sales Compensation." 2001.

Levy, Steven. "Facebook Grows Up." *Newsweek Magazine* (August 27, 2007): 40-46.

U.S. Bureau of the Census. November 2004, and May 2006.

LaVergne, TN USA
21 October 2010

201764LV00004B/4/P